HOPE
LIVES
HERE

HOPE LIVES HERE

ANGELA S. HATCH

AMBASSADOR INTERNATIONAL
GREENVILLE, SOUTH CAROLINA & BELFAST, NORTHERN IRELAND
www.ambassador-international.com

Hope Lives Here

ISBN: 978-1-62020-512-9
eISBN: 978-1-62020-418-4

Scripture references marked NIV are from The Holy Bible, New International Version®, NIV® Copyright © 1973, 1978, 1984, 2011 by Biblica, Inc.® Used by permission. All rights reserved worldwide.

Cover Design by David Fox and Hannah Nichols
Page Layout by David Fox and Hannah Nichols
eBook Conversion by Anna Raats

AMBASSADOR INTERNATIONAL
Emerald House
427 Wade Hampton Blvd.
Greenville, SC 29609, USA
www.ambassador-international.com

AMBASSADOR BOOKS
The Mount
2 Woodstock Link
Belfast, BT6 8DD, Northern Ireland, UK
www.ambassadormedia.co.uk

The colophon is a trademark of Ambassador

#908707961

DEDICATION & THANKS

This book is dedicated to all the hands and feet of Christ.

I would like to thank my family for all of their support, especially my husband, Jerry, who is my best friend, advisor, and favorite building buddy. And, a big thanks to my parents who have always been super supportive of all my crazy dreams, even that one about being a writer. Thanks to the Casas por Cristo crew who are the best missionaries ever, and thanks to Mrs. Lori Nij from Morning Glory, who shared her story and explained we are all "part of the story." She teaches the "brown-eyed children." Thanks also to Savannah Silver, Stacy Lee, and Trey Brakefield who provided some of the photos, showing us a view of Guatemala from their lens. Not only are they great to serve with, but they are also great photographers. And also, thanks to Henry Norton for his mad skills in Photoshop/photo conversion.

BACKGROUND

From the Casas por Cristo website:
"Located at the southern tip of México, Guatemala is the most populated country in Central America. With over 13 million inhabitants, 56% of the population is living in poverty. The majority of Guatemalans reside in rural areas outside of the bustling streets of Guatemala City. These mountainous country sides are where you will find the heart of this nation.

Rooted deep in its indigenous Mayan culture, it is typical to see the traditional dress worn by women and children as they carry belongings in baskets upon their heads. Produce stands line the dirt streets and small markets carry meat for purchase daily. The roads are typically filled with potholes, which turn into muddy pathways during the rainy season.

Many of the outlying villages are scattered with homes made of wood or bamboo and covered by rusty tin roofs. The inside of homes are typically sparse with only the most basic necessities; a fire pit to cook meals, ceramic jugs for holding water and mats woven from palms that are rolled out onto the dirt floor at night and used for sleeping.

Due to the lack of resources, women and children often suffer most from the poverty. Children are malnourished and forced to work to help provide for their family. With an already extremely high illiteracy rate, the problem continues to grow. Although many public schools are free, uniforms, books and transportation are still a required expense. Rather than learning in classrooms, many children spend their days rolling wicks for fireworks to help with the income. This job provides an average of 10 cents per 400 fireworks or 10 dollars for a full week of work. And although agriculture provides for 50 percent of the labor force, residents continue to struggle through seasonal labor on coffee, cotton and sugar plantations.

With adequate housing provided, families are relieved of one of their greatest financial struggles and a break is made in this vicious cycle. Children are given a hope for the future while parents can use their resources for food and necessities rather than shelter. As the American church partners with the Guatemalan church a perfect picture of the gospel is painted as cultures and nations are bridged together bringing about necessary provisions in the name of Christ."

CONTENTS

1

THE HILLS OF GUATEMALA

Rodrigo had never celebrated a birthday, but at what many would guess was the age of twelve, Rodrigo had only one dream: he wanted nothing more than to go to school. Nothing more than to learn to read so he could get a smart person's job. That's it; that's all he wanted. If he got a smart person's job, his family could have a better life; they could have dreams of their own.

Kristal, his older sister, couldn't have disagreed more. "Why would he want to go to school? We do not have time for that. We need to eat," she would say.

What does she know? Rodrigo kicked a pebble. It was early morning as Rodrigo held his hoe over his shoulder and headed off to work in the fields. This morning, however, Rodrigo's stomach felt funny, something was different. Maybe that's because Javi, his younger brother, asked him if everything was OK. Javi knew everything before anyone else ever did. He is very perceptive. Rodrigo didn't know what Javi was talking about and brushed off the comment.

Rodrigo chased the almost perfectly round pebble down the dirt path from his home, down the rutted street, and then down an alley that eventually led to the fields. He gave the pebble a good kick. It rolled further than he thought it would. When he caught up to the pebble, it had stopped in front of the gate to the Christian school. Rodrigo picked up the pebble and noticed how round it was and put it in his pocket, and then, without thinking, he checked the gate. It was locked. What am I thinking? I can't go in there. I need to be in the fields right now. He took his hand off the gate quickly as if it shocked him, and for the first time, he looked at his own hands—really looked at them. He noticed the callouses from the hard work he does in the fields. He noticed how rough and dirty his hands were and all the dirt under his nails. What am I doing here? He heard two boys in the distance and looked down the alley in their direction. They were kicking a soccer ball back and forth, getting closer, eventually passing Rodrigo. They nodded at him and thought nothing of him waiting at the gate. They just continued passing the old soccer ball with most of the leather worn off to each other. Neither one wore shoes. As they kicked the ball to each other, they pretended to be famous soccer players. One of the boys kicked the ball towards a free-roaming chicken. It squawked and moved out of the way. Rodrigo heard one of the boys say, "And he scores!" Rodrigo watched as the boys grew smaller and smaller and quieter as they got farther away.

To Rodrigo's left was a vast green field of tomatoes. The laborers were already in the fields working as the early morning sun poked through the clouds. Some of the women had small children strapped to their backs as they bent over to pick the vegetables. The field stretched as far as he could see. On the right were several shanties that looked much like the home he lived in. Walls were made of corn stalks woven together with twine and attached to four posts aligned in a square. The roof was flat and made of rusty, formerly discarded corrugated tin. A few sheets of two-by-eight tin were all that was needed to cover the whole home. Sometimes, if there were no walls, the homeowner used plastic sheeting to keep the rain from getting in and soaking the dirt floors.

"Good morning," said a voice from behind him. "Can I help you?"

Rodrigo spun around, completely startled. He saw a tall man looking at him. Rodrigo looked up at the man. His skin was very white and had light spots on it. His hair was cut short, above his ears, but even short, his wavy orange-red hair went everywhere. The man had a light beard like he had shaved a couple days ago. But even so, Rodrigo noticed it was very full and covered his whole chin. He remembered Tío, his uncle, had tried to grow a beard once, but it never covered his whole chin, so he stopped.

Caught off guard, he had not heard anyone approaching behind him. The man asked again, "Can I help you?"

Trying to gather his thoughts as quickly as he could, Rodrigo took a step back and stammered, "I . . . I . . . I. . . ." He paused as he tried to think of what to say. A million thoughts formed at once. *I should not still be here. Why am I here? I need to be a provider, I need to be in the fields like the others . . . but if I could read, I could be a real provider, and maybe Mamá could be healthy again.* Thoughts raced around in his head, and none of them were coherent; all he could do was blurt out, "I . . . I . . . I . . . want . . . to go to your school." Rodrigo was startled by the words that left his mouth. *Did I say that out loud?*

The man noticed Rodrigo had been waiting by himself. "Where is your mother, chico? Does she know you are here?"

Rodrigo held his breath and lowered his head. "My mother is not well, and she is not able to make this long walk." Rodrigo knew that was a stretch, and honesty was so important to Mamá. *Well, it is true.* But the larger truth, and the one he avoided, was his mother did not know he was there—and even worse, he was not sure his mother would approve of him being at the school. He should be in the fields working, she would say.

"She has bad lungs," said Rodrigo, shutting out the previous thoughts from his mind.

The man asked him some questions, many of which Rodrigo did not know the answers to. He could, however, answer the easy ones like "Where do you live?"

"I live about three kilometers that way, up over that second hill." He pointed towards the mountains.

But then the questions got harder, some he did not want to answer. "Does your mother know you are here?" Rodrigo noticed the man looking at his hoe. Silence. Rodrigo held his head down. He did not want to answer that.

"Who is your father?" He looked at Rodrigo. "How old are you, chico?"

Silence again. His nervousness began to rise. *Maybe I should have told Mamá.* He rubbed his hands on his pants. His hands were sweating. *I should not be here.* His mind was screaming.

"Your birthday. When is your birthday?"

Rodrigo tried hard not to show panic in his face, but he simply did not know. He no longer knew his father. His father left when Rodrigo's younger brother Javier was born. Rodrigo had been about six when that happened, so he didn't remember much of him anymore, other than what Mamá or Tío would say about him, but that was almost never.

How old I am? Rodrigo thought about that. "I don't know," he stated, like he hadn't thought much about that. "Birthday?" asked Rodrigo. "Sir, I'm sorry, but I do not know what that is." Rodrigo had no idea when his birthday was or even what a birthday celebration was, as his family had never celebrated one. Holding his head down and now getting nervous that he was not able to answer all of these questions, Rodrigo wondered if anyone else could hear his heart pounding in his chest. *This is not going well.* Panic started to swirl around in his mind. He could tell the man, who was being very patient, wanted some answers. Rodrigo tried to calm himself. He thought of the other boys dressed in their school uniforms who walked past him as he worked in the fields every day. *They are going to school, and someday they will have a smart person's job. I want to have a smart person's job.* Rodrigo took a deep breath. *I've got to look smart, like I could be a good student.*

As if the man heard his thoughts, he put his hand on Rodrigo's shoulder. Rodrigo looked up at him.

"We'll get some of the other details later. Come on in," the man said with a warm smile.

As they walked past the metal gate, Rodrigo could see three cinderblock buildings that looked like classrooms.

"I think we can find room here for you. My name is Michael, but most people call me el Padre. I teach here. What is your name?"

Rodrigo sighed in relief. He knew the answer to that one. "Rodrigo, señor." He smiled at the man.

Then el Padre looked Rodrigo in the eyes and said, "You are welcome here, Rodrigo," extending his hand out for a handshake. As Rodrigo shook el Padre's hand, he could feel his nervousness slowly melting away. Feeling the man's firm grip, Rodrigo could tell he was an honest man too. Rodrigo's heart skipped, and he tried hard to control his emotions. *I am going to go to school! I am going to school!* On the outside, he was calm, or was trying to be, but on the inside, crazy emotions of excitement and happiness were dancing around in his mind. It showed; he was grinning from ear to ear.

El Padre chuckled at his excitement.

"Thank you!" Rodrigo said, as some emotion spilled out. "Thank you for this opportunity. I promise you that I will be the best student you have ever had."

El Padre looked at him and tussled his hair. "I have a feeling you might be right. I can't say I've seen a kid this excited for school in a long time. Come on in." He opened the gate for Rodrigo. "Let me show you around." He walked Rodrigo around the school area. As they approached the largest building, el Padre explained, "This is our main building. This is where we meet for larger gatherings and where all the students eat lunch. It can fit up to fifty people."

Rodrigo's eyes widened as they walked in. The first thing he noticed was the smooth concrete floor. His house did not have a concrete floor. Then he saw rows of tables with bench seats. The table at his house was used for many things, sometimes for eating but most times for sitting around making firecracker wicks. He noticed a shelf of books on one wall of the room. As Rodrigo took it all in, el Padre continued the tour. Pointing in front of them, he said, "That's the kitchen. And that room off to the side is the office." He gave Rodrigo a moment to look around. "The office doubles as our library." Noticing Rodrigo's gaze on the books, el Padre said, "Someday, you'll be able to read all those books, Rodrigo. Would you like that?"

Rodrigo took a deep breath and thought about how different his day had become. He was supposed to be in the fields right now. If it weren't for the rock in his pocket, he probably would not have stopped in front of the school. If the boys had not captured his attention, he probably would not have stayed in front of the gate. If he wouldn't have stayed by the gate, he would not have spoken to el Padre. *Funny how things work out.* "I would like that very much."

"I thought so. I bet there's a book in there about managing your own business. I get the feeling you would like that one."

Rodrigo smiled.

As they walked by the office, Rodrigo noticed an examination table on the far side of the office and looked at el Padre. "We share that space with the community doctor," el Padre explained. "It's just until we get the space built for the second office, which should be some time next fall. For now, it seems to be working out. The doctor is available on Mondays and Wednesdays and sometimes on Fridays, so on those days it gets a little more crowded around here."

"Do you smell that?" asked el Padre. Rodrigo could smell something cooking but could not place what it was.

"Yes, but it does not smell like corn tortillas. What is it?"

"I'll show you what they are cooking."

Rodrigo listened as el Padre spoke. He liked listening to him speak. Rodrigo could tell he was not from around here; his light skin and red hair were the obvious clues. El Padre spoke Spanish, but it sounded different. Since Rodrigo didn't know anyone from anywhere else, he'd never heard anyone speak with an accent. They walked towards the kitchen. Rodrigo could hear el Padre's work boots on the concrete. El Padre wore jeans and a dark-blue T-shirt that read I AM PART OF THE STORY. The dark T-shirt accented how white el Padre's skin was. It was the whitest skin Rodrigo had ever seen, but he had never seen skin color other than his own. He noticed many spots on el Padre's arms. Rodrigo must have gotten a puzzled look on his face. "Do you know what these are?" asked el Padre, noticing Rodrigo looking at them.

Rodrigo, almost getting nervous again, just shook his head no.

"These are called freckles. I have no idea why God made them. They must serve some useful purpose, but I've never known what it is." Moving ahead a little, el Padre continued the tour. "So, this is the kitchen." Rodrigo saw women mixing up something soupy and white in a big pot. "If students do not have a lunch to bring, the school provides mash. That's what you are smelling. It's very healthy for you and contains lots of vitamins." El Padre was going to explain that it helps to prevent malnourishment, but instead, just added that it helps students think better. "We'll get you some at lunch; you'll like it. It's kind of sweet. So, let's head over to your classroom."

As they walked through the main building to the next cinderblock building, they passed a dirt courtyard where the children played soccer. El Padre pointed to the building. "This one's your classroom. This building has students in first through third grade. The building over there is for all the other grades. Sometimes it goes from fourth to ninth grade, sometimes just to sixth grade. It just depends on who shows up for class."

As they walked into the classroom, Ms. Sharon was already teaching but stopped once they walked in. El Padre walked over to her and gave her a smile and friendly hug. They spoke in a different language than Rodrigo knew. Ms. Sharon looked much like el Padre in that her skin was very light, but she was several years older. Her blonde hair had highlights of gray peeking though. It reached past her shoulders and was pulled back in a short ponytail. She wore a long cotton skirt with a button-down, short-sleeved blouse.

As el Padre introduced them, Rodrigo could see the wrinkles around her eyes and could tell that she must smile a lot. Ms. Sharon shook Rodrigo's hand warmly and with a smile, said in Spanish, "Nice to meet you, Rodrigo. We are so glad you are here."

So am I. Rodrigo smiled back and shook her hand.

She leaned in and looked him in the eyes. "How old are you, son?" she asked.

He looked at el Padre, who answered for him.

"We're guessing he's around twelve."

"Well, twelve it is then. And you've never been to school before, right?"

Rodrigo shook his head no.

"Well then," she said, fanning her arm around the classroom, "welcome to first grade."

So, on that day, Rodrigo was the first in his family to ever go to school.

Ms. Sharon looked over to el Padre, and in English said, "He doesn't seem to talk much."

Though Rodrigo had no idea what she was saying, he sensed a slight concern in her voice. He put his hands in his jeans pockets and felt the round pebble in one pocket. The other pocket had a hole in it. He noticed the class was looking at him. He noticed they all had uniforms. Anxiety crept into his mind as he thought about how he was going to pay for a uniform. *One issue at a time.* He took a deep breath. Rodrigo knew if he could read, he could get a good job and provide for his family. Then he wouldn't need to work in the fields or make a meager living making firecracker wicks in order to support his family. *Someday, I am going to be smart and have a smart person's job.*

El Padre responded, also in English, "Give him time. I want to give this kid a chance. His mom is very sick." Then he added, "I think you'll like him. He's got a spark."

"Well, maybe once he talks, I'll see it." She smiled at Rodrigo.

Rodrigo wasn't sure if he should smile back or look at the class or look down at the floor. He fidgeted with the pebble in his pocket.

"You'll see," said el Padre. Looking at the students, he asked in Spanish, "What day is it, kids?"

"Tuesday!"

"That's right! That means I'll see you all in a little bit," he said, waving good-bye to the students.

Ms. Sharon introduced Rodrigo to the class. "Class, this is Rodrigo. I hope you all make him feel welcome."

In spite of feeling a little awkward at the start of class, Rodrigo felt very welcome. He recognized many of the other students, even though they were much younger than him. A few of them lived close to him and were the younger brothers or sisters of kids his age. Most of the other students were around six. There were a few kids that were a little older, but none as old as he was. He took a seat next to an open space on a long bench. Since he had no notebook or pencil, he just rested his hands on the table in front of him and listened as Ms. Sharon spoke. He learned about the sounds a letter makes and learned about numbers. He could already add simple numbers; that was something he learned from Tío.

Tío made sure Rodrigo could count well so he could barter fairly. "Bartering is not meant to take advantage of a person; it's to get a fair deal," Tío had explained. "So you must be honest and fair, but also you must know how to count."

After about an hour, el Padre walked back into the room, holding up a large ball. "Does anyone know what this is?" he asked. It was colorful and had lots of green areas and blue areas, and it could spin. Rodrigo had no clue what it was, nor did anyone else. No one had seen one of these before. "This is a globe," he explained. "A globe is what the earth looks like if one were looking at it from space. See how it spins? The earth actually spins all the time to give us night and day. When it rotates all the way around, that is a day. One rotation is a day. While the earth spins to give us day and night, it also rotates around the sun to give us our different seasons. Depending on where the earth is in relation to the sun, we will have rainy seasons, or winter, and sunny seasons called summer, when we plant crops." He spun the globe and the colors whirred around. He touched his finger tip to the globe; it stopped spinning. "All these green areas are land. Each one is a continent and in each continent, there are many countries. All of the green areas are different places in the world where people live. See this area here?" he said, pointing to a small patch of green touching lots of other green patches. "This is your country. Guatemala." Moving his finger to the lower part of the green patch, he added, "And this spot right here is about where we are right now." The students leaned forward, trying to see. After they all had a look, he spun the globe again, stopped it with his finger, and looked where his finger rested. "Africa. Has anyone ever heard of Africa? In Africa, there are many jungles, much like the jungle in northern Guatemala. They have elephants and lions. Your country does not have them. Instead, you have monkeys and beautiful birds in your jungle areas. In Africa, people live in tribes, and they speak the language of their tribe. There are many languages in Africa."

El Padre spun the globe in front of Rodrigo and motioned for him to stop it with his finger. Rodrigo put his finger out, and it touched the bumpy surface. As he pressed his finger in slowly, the spinning stopped. "Oh look," said el Padre, "it's the United States. That is where I am from. In my country, most people speak English. Ms. Sharon speaks English too, but she is from a different country. It is called the United Kingdom, or England." He moved his finger across the blue area, the Atlantic Ocean, then pointed to another green spot on the globe, England.

Rodrigo never thought much past the dust and tin of his home or the fields where he worked. Never thought much about anyone else other than those in his pueblo. He would see stars at night, but never thought that another boy around the world could be looking at the same stars that he saw. If he saw that boy, what would he be thinking? Rodrigo sat, enthralled as el Padre spoke of other lands. Class ended, and the other children gathered their few belongings and headed out the door. Rodrigo kept staring at the globe, thinking about what it would be like to live in another land.

El Padre walked up to Rodrigo. "What did you think of your first day of school?"

"It was the best day of my life. Thank you very much for allowing me to come here."

"Sure," he said with a smile. "I know you will do well here."

El Padre walked him out of the classroom. "Oh, I just remembered," he said as he reached into his satchel. "I think you might be able to use these." He pulled out a pair of khaki slacks and a white shirt. "Check them out to see it they fit."

Rodrigo's face lit up. "Thank you! That is very kind of you." He held the pants up to his waist. They overlapped at the floor. "Perfect. Maybe just a little long, but I can fix that." He cradled the pants under his arm.

As they walked out together, el Padre added, "I did some homework of my own. Turns out I know where you live. In two weeks, a missionary team will be coming to build a home just down from yours. I will get to meet your family."

Rodrigo shook el Padre's hand again. "Thank you again." He left happy as he walked home. Lost in thought of light skin, red hair, mash, cement floors, spinning globes, and places that other people in the world lived, Rodrigo's thirty-minute walk home seemed to last just a mere couple of minutes. He was abruptly snapped out of his thoughts when he saw Kristal.

"What have you done, Rodrigo?" asked Kristal, his older sister. Her eyes had a fire in them. He knew this was not going to go well. Her friend Marissa had told her Rodrigo had come to the school that day. "What will Mamá say when she finds out?" She stoked the fire to the cooking stove. Smoke filled the area. Rodrigo could feel the heat from the fire and backed up a little. Kristal had been preparing masa, a type of dough made from ground corn, for the tortillas they would have for dinner.

"When she finds out?" Rodrigo's mind was churning as they stood by the fire. "She will be happy that I will learn how to read. She will know that I am doing this for our family, Kristal. She will know that one day, I will provide us a home of our own."

"No, Rodrigo!" Accustomed to the heat, Kristal flipped the hot tortillas with her fingers. "Our family needs us to work. How are we to eat?" Her voice started to get a little louder, her anger a little more pronounced. "We do not have the freedom of dreams. Those are silly thoughts."

"Freedom of dreams?" Rodrigo raised his voice. "What is bad about dreams, Kristal? Those are my dreams. What is so bad wanting to live—"

Kristal put her finger up to her lips. "Shhhh." They could hear Mamá coughing. She was resting on a pallet in the sleeping area, just on the other side of the sheet of plastic that served as a makeshift wall. She listened to see if Mamá's cough worsened and was relieved to hear it subsided.

Still angry, he whispered loudly, "What is wrong with wanting to provide Mamá with a nice house? A house where she won't have to sleep on muddy floors during the rainy season. A house that will block out the smoke from the cooking fire. A house where she will be able to get healthy again, so she can breathe better. Don't you want Mamá to get better?"

"Oh, Rodrigo, you are so full of dreams. Once Mamá finds out—"

"Finds out what?" Mamá asked curiously. Startled by their mother's voice, both Rodrigo and Kristal jumped when they saw her standing behind them.

2

THE OPTIMIST, THE PESSIMIST, AND THE NEGOTIATOR

Javier was six years younger than his brother, Rodrigo, but as the youngest, he was not the "baby of the house" because they also lived with their younger cousins, ages one and two. They all lived together—Rodrigo, Kristal, Javier, along with Tío and his wife, their two baby cousins, and Mamá—all of them together in a small plot etched out of the mountains of Guatemala. Papá left after he found out Javier was crippled. That was six years ago. That's also when they moved in with Tío, Mamá's brother. Their uncle has been the father they no longer have. They all lived under the same roof. No interior walls, just one large room. The one large room is where they all slept on separate pallets on a dirt floor.

Their casa was mostly made of bamboo connected together with twine, and a nailed-on tin roof. One wall was made of heavy, black plastic. That was the "door" wall. Rodrigo brought it back one day after working in the fields. Farmers use the black plastic around the plants in the fields to reduce the amount of dirt that gets on the vegetables. By doing that, there are fewer imperfections in the crop, which brings a higher price. The farm owner said Rodrigo could have the plastic scraps when they were done making rows in the fields. This made Tío very happy, because that plastic would provide a little more protection in the casa now that the rainy season was starting. The bamboo walls did not offer much protection against the rain, even if the pieces were tied together closely. Tío hung the plastic and it rustled in the wind, making muffled, crackly noises. Now that the "door" wall was hung, they would stay a little drier. Water would still stream through the ground at their feet during a big storm, but it provided a little more protection. And "a little more is better than none at all," says Javier.

Javier was the optimist in the family. But out of the three of them, he would be the least likely. Javier had the biggest reason *not* to be optimistic. He was born with one leg normal and one leg crippled. Some say it was because Papá raised his hand to Mamá when Tío wasn't around to stop it; others say it was just God's will. Whatever the case, Javier barely noticed it anymore.

"What Javier lacks in strength," says Tío, "he makes up for in optimism and intellect." Tío, who acts more like a father figure to Javier than an uncle, likes to bring Javier with him when he barters at the market.

"Javier, you are very perceptive. You can tell if someone is being honest or not," he said once when Javier was younger. "I remember when we went to the market to get a pig. Do you remember that, Javi?"

Javier loved stories that his Mamá and Tío told him. He listened to them tell stories as they all rolled firecracker wicks. Javier helped Mamá and Tío and Kristal make firecracker wicks during the day

The whole family participates in rolling wicks for fireworks. They typically receive about 100 quetzales, which equates to about $10.00-$12.00/week.

while Rodrigo worked in the fields. Firecracker wicks are about a foot long. Wicks contain one fuse, lined with gunpowder, and three pieces of long, thinly shredded newspaper wrapped around the fuse. Each wick is rolled and twisted, then stacked in a bundle to be taken to the firecracker factory a couple times a week. The wicks will eventually be inserted into large fireworks that are used to make beautiful fireworks displays at big celebrations.

Rolling the strands of string lined with gunpowder and wrapping them around strips of newspaper was how Rodrigo's family made their living. That was how many families in the area made their living. Because Kristal, Rodrigo, and Javier did not go to school, Tío taught them to count. It took four hundred wicks to make a bundle, so they could count to four hundred with ease. With each bundle, they could make ten cents. In a good week, they could make ten dollars.

Twice a week, Tío would bring several bundles to the factory in town where they made great displays of fireworks. Because it was too heavy to carry a week's worth of work in one trip, Tío would make two. He wrapped the bundles up in a colorful Mayan carrying cloth, tied the edges into a knot, and rested it on his forehead as the weight of the bundles rested on his back. Usually Javier would join him on the walk and sometimes they would stop by the market to see any new wares made by the locals. Javier liked making wicks for fireworks be- cause he loved to see what beau- tiful fireworks his wicks would produce. Javier took great pride

Twigs gathered for trade. Carrying items on heads and backs is typical of Guatemalans.

in his work. Other than just being perceptive, it was the only thing he felt he was good at.

Recalling the pig story, Javier nodded to Tío. He remembered the story and the day very well. It was a cloudy day, much like it was that day. Because it was cloudy, the area was foggy early in the morning, and it was very difficult to see. The air was thick and Mamá found it harder to breathe on those days. Rodrigo was getting ready to go to the fields, but could not find his hoe. As he searched the area, he realized where he left it from the night before, but it had been knocked over sometime during the night. Eventually, he found it, but only after he stepped on the blade, and the handle came up and popped him in the head. When he screamed, he woke Tío, who ran out with his machete to protect the family from the in- truder. Rodrigo came very close that day to needing stitches. But the way Tío protected his family, Rodrigo would not only have needed stitches, but probably also a cast.

After that happened, the next morning Tío said, "Javi, I think we need a pig to help guard the house. We can use it for food once we fatten it up." Javi loved going to the market to see all the things people sold. Once they arrived, a man approached them and asked if they wanted to buy his pig. Tío looked the pig over. "Looks good to me," he said without hesitation, still thinking how close he had come to possibly hurting Rodrigo earlier that morning. The thought still haunted him. Tío looked at Javier and waited for him to shake his head yes. Surprised when Javier shook his head no, Tío almost bought it anyway, but knowing that Javier was very perceptive, he decided to follow Javier's instincts.

"No pig today," said Tío, looking questioningly at Javi. After they left the area, Tío asked Javi why they didn't get the pig.

Javi said, "I don't know. It just didn't feel right." The man selling it was disappointed. They found out the next week when they went back to the market that the pig died from a disease.

"Javi, I will never go to the market again without you," said Tío. It does not seem to bother Javier much that he is not like all the other six-year-old boys—that he can't run and play and jump around. Not able to play with the other boys and girls, Javier has become an expert at making wicks and can roll wicks as fast as Tío if he concentrates. Mamá likes it when Javier helps. Mamá tells Javier stories of when she was a little girl, when she was healthy.

In spite of his crippled leg, Javier always seemed happy. Kristal did not share the same optimism or perception as Javier and wondered why he seemed so content with his lot in life. She wondered

Using a flat stone and soap stick, this young mother does the laundry daily to clean the few clothing possessions she has.

why, in spite of his crippled leg, he always seemed so optimistic and happy. The sky is always sunny to him.

"How does he do it?" Kristal asked Mamá one day when they were washing clothes.

"Do what?" asked Mamá.

"How is it that Javi is always happy? How can he be happy all the time?"

"Some people are just like that," replied Mamá. "Everyone loves to be around happy people." She rubbed a little bit of the laundry soap bar on the last shirt they were washing and scrubbed the shirt on the washing stone. Kristal finished rinsing and wringing out the pants Mamá had washed and waited for the shirt Mamá was working on. Mamá handed her the last shirt and added, "*You* could probably use a lesson there, Kristal." Then she sat down to rest, smiling.

Kristal didn't say anything as she rinsed and wrung out the shirt. Kristal knew Mamá was half joking, but her other half was telling the truth. "Happy is a choice," said Mamá. Slowly getting up, she added, "OK, we are done." Wiping her hands on her traditional Mayan dress, she stated, "I'm going to start the fire for dinner. Would you please get me some rice? We will have that with our tortillas tonight."

"Yes, Mamá."

Kristal got up also and prepared to "get rice." "Getting" anything meant bartering. Kristal looked around to see what they would barter and remembered Rodrigo had gotten some tomatoes earlier that day while working in the fields. Kristal moved the plastic sheet wall, and behind it was the stack of tomatoes resting on a ledge. "These are beautiful, Rodrigo. They will be perfect." She picked up five ripe and juicy red tomatoes perfect to trade for a bag of rice and put them in a basket, placed a cloth ring on the top of her head, then balanced the basket on top of her head. "Want to come with me?" she asked.

They left down the hill.

"Why do you not have dreams, Kristal?" Rodrigo asked.

"Because dreams are for people who already have food."

Rodrigo waved his hands dismissively. "No," he said emphatically. "I do not believe that. You have dreams inside. You just do not see them. They are there." They negotiated through the ruts on the path. "One day we will not have to look out of the holes in the tin roof to see the stars. We will see them through windows."

Kristal looked at him, almost as if he were crazy. *We do not have money for such dreams.* She almost interrupted, but she let him continue. She wanted to ask him just how he planned to get these windows and tin roof without holes when they barely had any food to eat.

"Someday we will no longer need to roll over on our sleeping mats to keep the water from dripping on our faces because of the holes in the tin. Someday, we will not have to sleep on the hard ground. It will be dry. Someday, Kristal. I mean it." Rodrigo had a sense of finality in his voice, a sense of desperation, a sense of *this is going to happen.* He held on to his hope. It was all he had.

No longer able to hold back her thoughts, Kristal said, "Rodrigo, you are loco. How can you think like that?"

"Think like that?" he repeated. "We *must* think like that."

Hope was something not many had in the hills of Guatemala. But Rodrigo had it. He knew in order to keep his dream alive, he had to hold on to this hope with all his might.

"We will never have a house like the one in your dreams," said Kristal. "You should not talk those crazy thoughts. Especially in front of Javi. He is too young for you to fill his head with this kind of talk. He just doesn't understand."

"Doesn't understand? Now, you are the crazy one. He is only six, but he is smarter than both of us! His crippled leg has nothing to do with his ability to understand. Kristal, you baby him. He wants to be strong."

"I know, but he will never be strong."

"Maybe you are right, but he doesn't need to know that. That is *his* dream, Kristal. Let him have that."

"You and your dreams, Rodrigo," she sighed. "We do not have time for such nonsense."

"We are fools if we believe any less," said Rodrigo. "You say you are a realist? A realist would know that we can change things if we try, Kristal. You are not a realist, you . . . you . . . are a pessimist!" His voice started to raise. The words stung Kristal.

"I am not a pessimist," she said defensively. They traded their tomatoes for the rice and brought it home to Mamá. Rodrigo and Kristal did not speak to each other the rest of the night. Dinner was quiet. Javier could tell something was wrong, but he did not ask.

"Checkers?" he asked Tío after they ate. Anticipating a yes, Javi unrolled the cloth "board" and lined up the rocks to play.

"Sure."

3

THE SMOKE

Kristal woke up early and could smell the smoke from the cooking fire. Through an opening in the plastic tarp that formed the doorway, she could see her mother starting the cooking fire for the morning breakfast of corn tortillas. Mamá fanned the smoke away, but the air was thick, and the overcast day did not allow the smoke to escape easily. Between fanning, Mamá coughed as the smoke tightened in her lungs.

As Kristal sat up, she noticed Rodrigo was not there. Kristal ran out to the cooking fire where Mamá was and said in a very loud whisper, "Mamá! Mamá! Rodrigo is gone! He is not inside!"

Mamá detected the panic in Kristal's voice. "He is fine, Kristal. He is in the fields." Seeing the confusion in Kristal's expression, she added reassuringly, "He is a very good negotiator, Kristal." Then Kristal knew Mamá and Rodrigo must have talked.

"Are you angry that he is going to school, Mamá?"

"Angry? No, sweet girl, I am not angry." Kristal went over to her and gave her a morning hug. She brought her hairbrush over to Mamá. "I cannot provide for my family as well as I would like to, so I pray his dreams will come true. I want him to go to school and grow up to be smart." Brushing Kristal's long hair, Mamá began to put it in a ponytail. "Rodrigo made me a promise. He said 'Mamá, I do not think sleeping on a dirt floor is healthy for you, so I want to help. I want to get you a new house. But I cannot do that until I can get a job for a smart person. And I cannot do that until I first learn to read. So, Mamá, can I go to school'?" Mamá took a breath that turned into a cough. "Isn't that just like him?" She smiled.

"So what did you say?" asked Kristal, a little surprised, as she was expecting her to not approve. She looked at Mamá to make sure she was okay from the coughing and waited for her response.

"Like I said, he is a good negotiator. He promised me he would work in the fields every morning for two hours before going to school. How could I say no?"

The next morning, Kristal sat up and again panicked when she did not see Rodrigo. Then she recalled her talk with Mamá the day before and relaxed. *He is fine.* She remembered that Rodrigo was in the fields. She rolled over in her pallet and smiled. *He is quite the negotiator, isn't he?* Even after two weeks, Kristal still had a hard time adjusting to Rodrigo not being there when she woke up. Kristal always woke up first—first, that is, after Mamá.

Rodrigo held up his part of the deal. He would get up early every morning to work in the fields, just as he promised, and then go to school. In the evenings, he would tell everyone what he had learned. Mamá would just laugh at him. Rodrigo was so excited about being in school. Kristal liked that it made Mamá smile, and Javi liked that he was getting "smart" too. For the first time in a long time, Kristal noticed there was happiness at dinnertime. After they ate, Mamá, Tío, and Tía, their aunt, would drink their coffee while everyone was still gathered around the fire, and they all would listen to Rodrigo's stories from school.

As Kristal awoke, the early morning sunlight streamed into the room and mixed with the smoke that was wafting in the air. It made an interesting image as the sunlight cut through the smoke. Kristal extended her arms in a stretch, and when her arms touched the dirt floor, she leaned back and looked around. Still trying to wake up, she saw the bare spot where Rodrigo slept. Next to her, Javier was sleeping peacefully. As Kristal leaned over to get up, the blanket moved, and she could see the contours of his crippled leg in the shadows. She covered him back up to let him sleep.

Kristal got up to fold her sleeping pallet and noticed Mamá's cough got louder. "Good morning, Mamá. Your coughing seems bad today. How do you feel?"

"I was hoping for blue skies today, but still, I am well."

Kristal knew when the skies were blue, the humidity was lower, which made breathing much easier for Mamá. Kristal looked up and saw mostly overcast clouds and knew it would be a difficult day for Mamá. She already sounded weak, and it was still early. Kristal knew Mamá wouldn't have much energy by noon.

The closest accessible drinking well to their pueblo was about three kilometers away and was especially treacherous this time of year due to the rainy season. The road, made of hard dirt and lined with pot holes and ruts, was difficult for anyone. But for the women and girls carrying water in large vases delicately balanced on their heads, it was a navigational chore. As the women made their daily

Catching up with the day's events, local ladies gather to talk while effortlessly balancing their loads.

trip, they would descend down the hill and the rugged area that had pot holes. After a few minutes, the ground would level off and they would go through a much more travelled road, a paved road. Being careful to avoid the vehicles and horses, the girls would turn down an alley, the same alley where Rodrigo first waited by the gate to go to school. She looked over to see if she could see him playing outdoors, but she wasn't sure if he was in the fields or at school at this time. Past the school and the fields, the girls could see some of the men walking towards the fireworks factory, the largest employer of the region. Tío sometimes joined the girls on their trip to get water while he went to the factory with his wicks. When they would arrive at the alley, they would go opposite directions. The fireworks factory was one way; the well was the other way. "I will wait

Local girl carrying tortillas to sell or trade.

for you girls here," he would say, as it was the halfway point between the well and the factory.

Kristal got ready to get water and picked up the water pot. "I am going to walk with Marissa today. I will not be gone long. I'll be back soon enough to help you with lunch." Tío was ready to go but did not join them today. "I am waiting for Javi to be ready to go. I may see you along the way."

Kristal hugged Mamá.

"Be careful. I feel a darkness in the air today," said Mamá with concern in her voice. "Be very careful."

"Yes, Mamá." Kristal hoisted her water jug to her head and walked towards Marissa's house. Because Kristal's mother suffered from a respiratory illness and couldn't make the treacherous walk, Kristal had to carry clean cooking water for the family daily. It was a chore she didn't mind as that was where she would see her friends, especially her best friend, Marissa.

Marissa lived a couple of houses down from Kristal. Their families often traded goods with each other. Rodrigo would bring squash, tomatoes, and cucumbers back from the fields that he would trade for coffee, beans, and corn. Marissa and Kristal were best friends, but there were some things Kristal did not understand about Marissa. Like school, for example. After their early-morning gathering of water, Kristal noticed that, lately, Marissa had been going to school instead of staying at her casa during the day. Even though Kristal spent most of her day at home rolling firecracker wicks with Mamá and Tío and Javier, Kristal missed taking some breaks and talking with her best friend or playing jump rope.

"Why do you go to that school?" asked Kristal, looking straight ahead as she balanced the pot on her head. "You know girls don't need an education." She watched her footing as they walked down the steep hill and continued, "When you get older, you will find a good man, get married, take care of the home, and have children." She added matter-of-factly, "You don't need an education for that."

"What do you mean, girls don't need an education?" Marissa was surprised that Kristal would ask such a question. Marissa, a slight step ahead of Kristal, tried to look back, but moving her head would have upset the delicately balanced water jug on her head. And especially since they were on the hill, it would have been difficult to stop, so she continued going down the hill looking straight ahead. "Everyone needs an education," she said, wondering why Kristal even brought it up. She repeated Kristal's question. "Why do I go to the school?" She rebalanced the water pot on her head. "The school is wonderful. I feel good when I go. I learn things. Things that will make me smart. El Padre is very smart, and I want to be just like him. He tells us things that make me think about my future and about hope."

Since Rodrigo started going there, he has been talking the same nonsense, thought Kristal. "First Rodrigo, and now you? He says the same thing. Why do you talk such nonsense?" she asked.

"It is not nonsense. El Padre says if we have hope, we have life."

"That is what Rodrigo says," replied Kristal, frustrated. "I think he is loco." Dressed in a traditional brightly colored Mayan dress, Kristal's long black hair blew in the wind. She pulled her hair behind her. Kristal's deep-brown eyes made her look much older than her thirteen years. As they got up to the well, Marissa filled up her large vessel and waited for her best friend to finish filling her own vessel. Kristal put her jug under the running water. Hope. Kristal let the word float around in her head as she filled up her water jug. She did not like the word "hope." She thought about one of her neighbors, who once spoke to her about hope.

"Maybe Maximón [pronounced maa-shee-MOHn] could help cure your Mamá," the neighbor suggested. "Remember when little Carlita was very sick?" Carlita's Mamá had gone to Maximón to ask him to cure her. "Little Carlita is healthy now. And you know Humberto from down the street? He did not have a job for three months. He got a job the next day after he visited Maximón. The same thing happened with Paco. It took him only a week. Maximón can help your Mamá too," she said in a helpful tone. "I know you want her to feel better."

Kristal knew who Maximón was. He was the Mayan God many of the indigenous worshipped. He was the one they rested their hope on. If he could listen to all of them, maybe he would listen to me, she thought. Mamá is so sick. It is so hard for her to breathe. With resolve, she thought, I will go.

Kristal took the bus the next day. It took two fares to get there, but it was very easy to find. After walking to the outskirts of the neighboring pueblo, she found the Maximón in the Mayan temple. The shrine was located at one end of the pueblo, as far away as possible from the Catholic church on the other end. When Kristal approached the shrine, she saw the shaman in front of the entrance. On a mission, she walked through the parking lot towards the stairs. She was determined to help her Mamá to get better. She saw the shaman up close. She knew that Mayan shamen are considered by many to be the link between evil spirits and good spirits. He offered hope for those who did not have any. Kristal saw his headpiece tied with a headband. It was a simple brown color, as long as his hair. He was

Maximón at the temple

standing by a smoky fire, hovering over a young man. She heard him say something about how his spirit was now cleansed. She passed some egg shells smoldering in ashes, stacked in a little pile just before the stairs to enter, an offering left by someone who probably already entered.

As Kristal entered the temple, she felt a tingle up her neck and heard a voice in her head, "You should not go there. It is evil." She went in. It was dark. Her eyes had to adjust to the lack of light, and as she waited to see better, many smells wafted in the air, hitting her all at once.

In front of her were several metal tables with candles of different colors burning on them, each one representing a different request. Red was for love. Green was for hope and good outcomes on business negations. Pink was for health. Black was for getting rid of enemies. There were many colors of candles lit. As they burned down to nothing, pools of different-colored wax started to mix. I should look for a pink candle, thought Kristal.

Maximón was seated on a wooden chair at an altar in the front of the shrine, wearing a black suit, red tie, and bowler's hat. His clothes were stuffed with newspapers to help prop him up as he stared straight ahead from his paper-mache face. He had a dark mustache and was covered by a clear sheet of plastic. A man from the pueblo was in front of him, making his petition to Maximón. The man gave Maximón a cigar and splashed rum on him, then placed the rest of the bottle on the altar at Maximón's feet. A line of people flanked along the wall, waiting for their turn to give Maximón their offer-ings of spices, rum, and money in exchange for an answered petition.

What is all this? How is this hope? Kristal thought maybe she should have listened to that voice she heard when she first walked in. She thought she should not be here; she did not like this kind of hope. Kristal had no money and no offerings to give. She barely had the bus fare to get here. She just had a prayer. All she wanted was for Mamá to feel better. Kristal stood by the pink candle, lit by someone previously, and thought of her Mamá. The smell of spices and alcohol and incense was overwhelming, giving Kristal a headache like she had never felt before. She began to get a sense of evil all around her and started to get dizzy. She left without making any petitions to Maximón. Since that day, she has not liked the word "hope."

Marissa spoke after the long pause. "Kristal . . . hello," she said, bringing Kristal back to their discussion by the well. "I do not think Rodrigo is loco at all. He really likes the school. If you do not have hope," Marissa said, "you have nothing. That is what el Padre says."

"Hope. I do not like hope."

They put the ring used to balance the jugs on their heads, then hoisted their water-filled vessels up to their heads and started on the trek back home.

"Before Rodrigo started school there, he was not loco," said Kristal. "He did not think such foolish thoughts."

"They are not foolish thoughts."

"Not foolish thoughts? It's all he talks about."

"That is great. Then maybe, someday, between him and me, you will finally understand."

"Never. I do not believe in hope," said Kristal, "I have seen hope. I don't want people to think I am crazy."

"Crazy? No. Stubborn? Yes."

There wasn't much more to say as they headed to the outskirts of the pueblo towards their home.

"Hey, is that your Tío?, asked Marissa.

"Yes, he was going to go to the fireworks factory this morning." Kristal waved to him and Javi.

Maneuvering their way along the road and through the ruts, the walk was quiet. It allowed Kristal to process some of her thoughts. Her discussion with Rodrigo the night before was still bothering her. She wanted to talk to Marissa about it as she was her best friend, but Kristal was not sure she wanted to hear the truth.

Feeling brave, Kristal asked, "Marissa, do you . . . do you think that I am a pessimist?"

Marissa did not respond; silence revealed her answer.

Kristal had started walking slower and began to sulk. *I am not a pessimist. I can't be. I have to be positive for Mamá. She needs us.*

The other girls who were also at the well had passed them. Marissa slowly turned around to see where Kristal was. "Are you coming?" she asked.

Kristal pretended her sandal was caught in a rut. "Yes, yes, I am coming."

Marissa looked at her, knowingly. "You are not a pessimist." She looked at Kristal and smiled. "At least not all the time." Marissa had a feeling that something was on Kristal's mind by the way their conversation went earlier. Normally, Kristal didn't seem so stubborn. "People might think you are a pessimist because you only think about today. You never think about the future."

"The future? What future?"

"See, there you go, you pessim—" She did not finish her word. It was drowned out by a loud, deafening noise. The explosion shook the ground around them. The thunderous noise echoed off the trees in the valley, nearly causing the girls to stumble and spill their water.

"What was that?" asked Kristal. But they both knew what just happened.

"No." Helpless, Marissa almost whispered, frozen in place. "Not again."

"We must go."

"I can't." Marissa was paralyzed as the noise replayed images that were burnt in her memory from two years ago. She could feel the pressure in the air, pressing against her ears, just like before. Her world began to echo. Everything was in slow motion. She could not bring herself to turn around. She started to shrink in posture, feeling like she was going to slowly crumble. "This cannot happen again." Kristal looked in the direction of the noise and saw the smoke. It sounded exactly as it had two years ago when there was an accident at the fireworks factory.

Kristal reached out for Marissa. "You cannot cry. You must be brave. We've got to go there. We must go and help." Kristal reached for Marissa's hand. Her hand was shaking, her body was shaking. "Marissa, we have to go there. We have to help."

Marissa slowly took Kristal's hand. They walked at first, then ran towards the fireworks factory and the smoke. Kristal heard another voice and remembered what her mother had said earlier that morning: "I feel a darkness in the air." And a chill ran down her spine.

4

CALLED TO COME

The weathered school bus stopped at the end of the pathway, at the bottom of the mountain. In its prime, it had served School District 728 in the United States. Since then it had been shipped to Guatemala, refurbished a few times, and bought by the organization Casas por Cristo. It's been on its last leg several times over.

Sixteen people streamed out of the bus, carrying backpacks, tools, and water jugs. Acting on obedience, they were all "called" to come. "The site is up this way, guys," said the site leader, pointing up the mountainous trail. "Go up to the area where you see a break in the fences, and turn left. You will see the site straight ahead. You'll know it because it's been leveled and cleared. That will be the future home of the García family."

On the hillside, areas of land were carved out of the side of the hill and leveled out, just large enough to put up some form of construction, usually tree limbs with bamboo and plastic, but sometimes cinder block. "I can't believe they actually build houses right on the mountainside," said one person on the team to the other as they hiked up the steep dirt pathway to the site.

"I can't believe they walk up this pathway every day," said the other, breathing hard. Not used to the altitude and steep climb, sweat was already beading down her face. Wiping her face, she could also feel sweat from her legs starting to roll down her calves. "Whew. I need to catch my breath."

Passing skinny dogs with blue collars and lots of curious faces peeking out from the bamboo-walled shanties along the way, the first of the team called out, "I see it! It's right up here!"

The site had already been prepared. It was flat and ready. The family had worked hard to level the ground where the house would be built. The ground, hard as rocks, had been difficult to level, but they had done the best they could with only a shovel and a pick ax. Off to the side was a stack of various kinds of lumber required for the home, some piles of rock and sand, and a couple of fifty-five gallon drums for water.

The García family saw the team as they approached. All eight family members were gathered around each other, some sitting on the ground, others on chairs or makeshift chairs. There was a folding chair, a small green plastic child's chair, and a few tree stumps gathered around in a circle, with only one being used at the time. The oldest daughter was trying to get her baby to finish eating, while also trying to comb her toddler's hair, but because of all the new faces starting to arrive, neither of the babies was cooperating as their mother would have liked. A breakfast of tortillas and eggs was now complete, or as complete as it was going to be.

The father of the house wore dark work pants and a light blue button-down, short-sleeved shirt. It had a logo that read BUDDY'S PLUMBING SUPPLIES sewn on the right and the name RALPH embroidered on the left. He was not Ralph or Buddy; his name was Juan de García, and since they did not have running water, it was a sure ringer that he knew nothing about plumbing. Weathered from the work he did outdoors in the fields as a farmer, his face revealed the lines of an older man, older than his actual age, somewhere in the early forties. Holding a cup of coffee, he finished the last of his breakfast as the team approached. He smiled at the team, but quietly stayed off to the side, eager to help. He had two gold teeth, and when he smiled he had evenly spaced wrinkles all down his face, starting from his eyes to the dimples on his cheeks.

The mother wore traditional Mayan clothing, a brightly colored woven dress with a woven apron. Her long, black hair was pulled back into a bun. A few strands of hair escaped the bun and blew in the light breeze. No shoes. None of the family wore shoes, except the father and older son. They had rubber boots. The mother stood up as she saw the builders arrive, folding her hands in front of her. Her face showed a life that had been hardened by the elements. As she stood by their "kitchen," an additional lean-to shanty separate from the sleeping area, she watched the stream of people hike up the hill. Excitement was hard to see from the outside, but from the inside, her heart was beaming. A fire smoldered outside the shanty, with a blackened sooty metal coffeepot on a rack keeping the coffee warm. She was still holding the old rag she used to get the coffee pot off of the bent rack without getting burnt. Excited for this day, she smiled, revealing a missing front tooth.

The two younger boys, Carlos and Pedro, under the watchful eyes of their mother, had gotten up to play with the other kids in the area. For a brief moment, they stopped playing so they could see new arrivers. The neighboring kids and the two younger boys mixed together, making it difficult for the team to know who was in the family and who the neighbors were. But at this moment, no one played. All eyes were locked on the new arrivers. Look at their pale skin, they all thought.

The oldest son, Roberto, normally gone to the fields by this time, was finishing up his last tortilla. When they found out they were going to be the next family to get a home, he helped the boys understand the concept of time in order for them to know when the big day would come. He had them gather several small rocks and put them in a stack next to the cooking fire. "When all the rocks are gone from this pile, we will have a new home." The days slowly ticked by for everyone.

When breakfast started, Carlos said, "Today is the big day. Right, Daddy? There are no more rocks in the pile."

"That is right, son." They had been anxiously waiting for this day to arrive, and the day had finally come. It was the day their prayers would be answered. Everyone was excited.

When news arrived that they would be the next family to get a home, Juan de García, the father of the house, openly cried. It

Local kids gathered up to play

was the second time in his adult life that he had done that in front of his children. The first was when they buried their twin baby girls who had died due to sickness, eleven years ago, to this day. This day was normally a sad one for the family, but on that day, it was one of their happiest. They had seen other families

Every morning, we passed this family and they greeted us cheerfully. This was the inspiration for this book. As we passed them by every morning, we wondered what they were thinking. How is it they look so happy when their neighbors were the ones getting the house? Padre answered it simply, "It gives them hope."

in the area get a home, and even though all of the families here had hard lives, and no one deserved it any more than the other, Juan was so excited they were the ones chosen for the next house. The García's had prayed for this day for many years, prayed that God would bless them. Juan knew God had blessed him with children and good work, but right then, that day, God had blessed them with a home.

Javier dropped the firecracker wicks he was rolling when he heard the people approach. He peeked around the black plastic sheet, and his eyes widened. Excitedly, he said, "Kristal! Kristal! Look! The people are here! They have come here to build homes! They are going to build casas, Kristal!"

Kristal walked over to Javier and rested her arm on the support beam, a weathered, old cedar post, and pulled back the plastic sheet to take a peek. She saw the people coming up towards them. "Javi, look how light their skin is," she whispered, almost in awe; they had never seen anyone like that. Looking down at her arm, she noticed her skin was very tan in comparison. *Where did they come from?* she asked to herself.

One person from the team came towards them and said good morning. As Kristal pulled herself closer to the support beam and used it to guard herself from the new face, he asked, "¿Cuantos niños aquí?" (How many kids here?) Kristal stared and shyly held out three fingers. Kristal recognized his Spanish words even though her family and all those around her mainly spoke K'iche', a Mayan language common to the central highlands region. Digging into his pockets, he found three pieces of hard candy and handed them to her. She took them and smiled, still very shyly. Javier peeked out from behind her to see what she held in her hand. She gave him a piece of candy, took one for herself, and saved the last one for Rodrigo. As they sucked on the hard candy, their eyes were glued to the building site just above them where their neighbors lived.

Resting from the hike up, the team waited for everyone to make it up the steep climb. They were all breathing heavily from the walk up the steep hill; some had already started sweating, partly from the walk, partly from the elevation. They gathered around the site, looking around to get a quick glimpse of their surroundings—a mixture of beautiful, luscious mountain views, contrasted with the dirt, rusting tin, and poverty. Once everyone was up the hill and gathered

To begin the day, the team gathers to pray for the build, the house, and the family. They encourage the family to join in. What a beautiful sound to hear praying in a couple of languages and to know that God knows and understands all that is asked and said!

around, the site leader said, "Let's form a circle. We're going to have a quick word of prayer."

"What are they doing?" asked Kristal, eyeing them curiously as they looked on from a distance.

"I don't know," replied Javier, a little perplexed.

As the leader prayed for God's blessing over this area, the family looked anxiously from the side. There was a crowd of onlookers curiously observing the strangers either from the nearby ledge or from their own bamboo homes. Mandi, one of the members of the team, looked up from where she was in the circle and noticed all of the eyes looking at them. Once the site leader finished the prayer, they all broke into groups.

"I need someone over here to inventory." He looked at one of the team members, Mandi, and asked, "Do you mind counting everything? We need to make sure we have all of our materials."

"Sure," she said, taking the inventory list from him. Turning to her friend Julie, she quipped, "He obviously knows my skill level." The site leader laughed.

Mandi, now in her early thirties, had never held a hammer until the day she started to pack for this trip. She had borrowed her father's hammer, and she remembered him saying, "You know how this thing works, right?" as he handed it to her.

Mandi recollected her conversation with her father. "Well, I know the concept," she said, and they both laughed.

The site leader gave Mandi the list.

"Um, I'm not sure what some of these things are."

Julie took the list from Mandi. "You're hopeless. How have you functioned all your life?"

Local kids look on with curiousity and excitement at the building of the construction project.

Mandi smiled her cute little smile. "By my looks?"

"Hardly," Julie said jokingly. "How about I point to what you need to count and you count."

"That works."

The site leader continued, "OK, I need another team over here to frame out our foundation. And a team over here starting on framing walls." Like ants, everyone scurried to find a job. The site leader added, "If anyone doesn't have a job, or if you want to take a break, feel free to mingle with the family. Get to know them. Play with the kids. They're so excited you're here. Show them how much we care."

Julie looked at the list again. "See those boards over there?" she asked, pointing to the two-by-fours. "We need fifty-two of them."

"Got it." Mandi started to count, got to around forty-five, and then had to start over. Twice. "Ugh. People keep using them." People started getting some of the boards to build the formers for the foundation, and others were grabbing some for the walls.

"Well, we are building a house, you silly."

Ignoring her, she found them all. "Fifty-two!" shouted Mandi.

"Good job! I knew you could do it," said Julie. Meanwhile, she had already counted most of the other boards and other materials and crossed them off the list. "Did you see a box for electrical?"

"Yes, it's over there." Mandi pointed to the other side of the pile of wood.

"OK, then it looks like we have everything. Wait, did you see cement bags?"

"Uh . . . cement bags. No, I don't think so."

"OK, I'll let the site leader know. Want to take a water break? We'll find out where they need help after that."

"Sure," said Mandi, excited to take some pictures. "I'm going to head out this way." Mandi brought her camera, hoping to catch a few candid shots of "normal" life in the highlands of Guatemala. She took photos of the children playing, of the women going about their day, of the surroundings. As Mandi took photos of some of the children curiously looking on, she couldn't help but notice the look of happiness and joy. It was a simple, innocent, child-like joy—a joy not complicated by electronics and the continual plugged-in moments of a hectic life. Of her hectic life. Mandi wished she had that joy. She suddenly felt the baggage she was carrying with her own life and longed for that simplicity.

After Mandi took a photo, she soon realized that when she showed the digital image to the children, she could easily make friends. They

Member of the team showing the fascinated kids an image of themselves on her phone.

loved seeing images of themselves. As the children crowded around her and giggled, she was pretty sure they were saying, "Me next! Me next!" Children were crowded everywhere around her, hoping to be the next one she would photograph. They never tired of looking at images of themselves. "You are so handsome!" Mandi said, showing the boy his image. She was not sure how to say it in Spanish, but it didn't matter; as she showed the boy the image, he looked at it with amazement and smiled shyly. The kids were amazed at the magic gadget that showed a small picture of what they looked like.

El Padre came up to Mandi and introduced himself. "Hi. Are you like the Mamá Rotsi?"

Getting the joke, Mandi laughed. "Mamá Rotsi . . . Paparazzi. Pretty funny." Extending her hand towards his, she said, "Hi. My name is Mandi."

"Well, hi, Mandi. I'm Michael, but most people here call me el Padre. I help with the local pastors and also teach at the school. So, that's a pretty nice camera," he commented. "Are you a professional?"

"No, it's just a hobby, but I love taking photos. I can't get over how much they love getting their photos taken."

"Yeah, they love it. You know, this is probably the first time they are seeing what they look like."

"First time seeing themselves?" she repeated inquisitively. "What do you mean?"

"Well," he replied, sweeping his hand in front of him to show the poverty surrounding them, "as you can see by looking around, there's not much room for vanity here. No one has a mirror to see themselves."

"Wow." Looking around, she started seeing things from a different perspective. "I saw the poverty, but I never thought of that."

"So," he said with a smile, "you just gave them a little gift. A little piece of who they are."

Wanting to take a few more photos, she asked, "Can you help me translate?"

"Sure."

One boy jumped in front of her and grabbed her hand, gently pulling and guiding her closer to the other children. She guessed he was one of the boys who belonged to the family for which the house was being built. He pointed to two little girls. They were his cousins, el Padre explained. Mandi took their picture. "You both are so beautiful."

El Padre smiled at the girls and relayed Mandi's words in Spanish. Then, the boy led Mandi over to the rest of his family, still tugging at her hand. She took photos along the way. Some of the women shied away from the camera, but were just as curious as the children. When they saw their images, they often covered their mouths and timidly giggled. El Padre laughed; one of the women looked at the image of her friend and jokingly said something about being a movie star.

El Padre looked at Mandi and the little boy leading her around with his hand. "Looks like Pedro has taken a liking to you."

"He's a cutie."

The team met the family. They were building the house for Juan de García and Patricia, the father and mother, their four children, and two grandchildren. Pedro pointed out his family. He pointed to his two brothers. "Roberto." He pointed to the taller boy, then moved his finger to the shorter one. "Carlos." Mandi guessed them to be fourteen and five, with Pedro being around seven.

"Good guessing," said el Padre. "I never do well with that. You guessed their ages right on all three."

Pedro pointed out his older sister. "Maria. She has two babies, Claudia and Sofia."

Mandi thought she looked so young to have two children.

"She's twenty-one," said el Padre.

"Really? She looks all of fourteen," Mandi said to el Padre.

El Padre smiled. "I stopped trying to guess ages long ago. I stay out of trouble that way." She smiled back.

"She is married," explained Pedro, "but he doesn't stay here anymore." El Padre translated, and Mandi nodded her head. Losing interest in the conversation, Pedro left to go play with his friends. "See you later," he said.

Mandi waved good-bye and smiled. She got a great photo of him running towards his friends as he was looking back and waving to her. Mandi looked around. "This is sure going to be a full house," she said to el Padre. "Are they all going to sleep in this tiny house?"

"Sure."

Mandi wondered how they would do that. "Yeah, but there's eight people. They're all going to sleep in that house? It's really not that big."

"Yup. They'll just pull out their mats. There's plenty of floor space."

"Wow. My efficiency apartment is at least twice the size of what this house will be, and it's only me in my apartment. I thought it was pretty small, but it looks like a mansion compared to this."

El Padre nodded. "Things are a little different over here." He remembered thinking the same thing when he first arrived in

Guatemala. "It's actually a little unusual when there is no extended family either living together or nearby."

She tried to take it all in. "So, I noticed there aren't many men around. It's mostly just women and children."

"Most of the men are either working at the nearby fireworks plant or in the fields, or they've moved to the city and no longer stay with their families." El Padre and Mandi walked a little beyond the work site and could see everyone working at their jobs. "Sometimes the men bring money back for the families they left behind, and sometimes their families never see them again. The father of this family comes back every few days. He works a few towns over doing field work. It's the only work he could find in the area. He's here today, but I am not sure how much more we'll see of him this week."

The site was etched into a fairly flat part of the hillside. Behind the site where the new house would be built remained the original house, a four-sided structure of dried chutes of bamboo with a rusty tin roof. They walked over to this area. The roof extended from this structure towards the cooking fire, which Mandi took to be the "kitchen." Mandi noticed there were no walls in the cooking area, just posts holding up the roof. "This is typical of the area,

A very common representation of the area: tin walls in upper view, child on way to get water with jug on head, laundry drying and kids in the forefront playing.

and also one of the reasons for people in this area to have chronic lung problems," he said. "I know the family just below there," he added, pointing down the hill. "The oldest boy goes to our school. His mother has lung problems so bad that she can barely leave the area. Climbing these hills is just too hard on her physically."

Mandi looked at the roof of the "kitchen." "It's really smoky." She waved the smoke away so it wouldn't sting her eyes and lungs.

"This is how they cook everything," he said. "No microwaves here. The cinderblock 'stove' is their only source of cooking."

Mandi noticed the fire was still going from breakfast.

"They'll use this again for lunch," he continued. "If I were to guess, I'd say probably tomatoes and corn tortillas."

Mandi peeked inside the original house. Ripe tomatoes rested on a ledge as a chicken wandered around inside. There were no beds, just woven mats that were rolled up and stacked to one side of the dark room. Blankets and other clothing were hung up over a string line. The hard dirt floor had ruts in it from rain washouts and from where they swept it over and over.

Mandi looked at the family, then at all of their belongings. The only furniture around was already out by the fire—the folding chair, the green plastic chair and three tree stumps. Mandi saw an old wire spool for a table. The family had moved their chairs, or make-shift chairs, and sat around the table where they rolled firecracker wicks. They were talking. She saw a dresser that the family let the team use as a stand for their table saw. There was an old pink children's table and some plastic bowls and other things stacked alongside the "kitchen." That was all they had in the world. Mandi looked at all of it. *Sparse could hardly be used to describe the furnishings*, she thought.

El Padre walked with Mandi as she looked in the distance. "The land is so beautiful," she remarked. "It is such a contrast to the poverty around us."

"Yes," he agreed, as he deeply inhaled and took in the view. "You will notice a lot of contrast around here."

Mountains and valleys and lush, green views surrounded them. A little closer in their viewpoint, they could see crops etched into the mountain in a stair-stepped method used to maximize farming and minimize erosion on the mountainous land. It almost appeared checkerboard-like on the landscape.

Off in the distance, Mandi saw some of the women laboring in the fields with their babies, who were nestled and cocooned in blankets around their mothers' backs. Bringing her view to the mountain they were on, she watched the children playing. The mountainside was the playground for the children as they fearlessly ran barefoot up and down the steep terrain, oblivious of any danger and without fear of getting injured.

Local kids made their own fun-filled teeter totter using available supplies.

"I can't believe they're just running around here without any regard to the thought of getting hurt." Looking at el Padre, she said, "Wow, I think I've just become my mother. She always used to say, 'Be careful or you'll poke your eye out.'"

El Padre laughed.

Mandi looked over and saw some children playing in a tree. The trunk of the tree was about four inches in diameter with the larger lower limbs no larger than about an inch. One boy, about the age of five, was in the tree, while two other boys were shaking the tree left and right, slowly at first, then building momentum. As the tree swayed back and forth almost to a snapping point, the boys tried to "shake" him out, and all three of them started laughing. Eventually, the tree slowed, and he jumped down. Showing his muscles and a big grin, the next boy got up for his turn.

El Padre chuckled. "You just gotta laugh."

Mandi pretended to cover her eyes. "I can't watch this. It makes me nervous."

"Yeah, you'll notice that safety is sometimes an afterthought around here. But, this is how the kids learn to balance and test their physical boundaries. It's pretty natural when you think about it."

"I still can't watch it."

Carlos wore a stained T-shirt with an image of a cartoon truck on the front with words I ONLY GO **FAST**. That pretty much explained him. His jeans, hand-me-downs from his older brother Pedro, were too big, and he pulled them up every few minutes. Pedro, dressed about the same in a T-shirt and torn jeans, was a natural leader and led them in their follies. With jet black hair cut short and bare feet with caked-on dirt, their tufts of hair would stand straight up as they ran.

They played with the exuberance typical of Guatemalan boys. With Carlos at his heels, Pedro pushed a plastic riding horse to the edge of the hillside and got ready for the ride. The faded brown and pink plastic horse was missing one of its wheels, and as they descended down the hill, the wheel-less leg would make a treacherous catapult when it speared the ground. Flying in the air, the boys squealed and giggled in a way that only an experienced, fearless child would enjoy. Mandi could barely watch for fear of their breaking an arm or a leg. Their innocent, simple life reminded her how complicated her life had become. As a thirty-something, rising executive, she started to see life through different lenses in her twenties, and somewhere along the way, her life choices and priorities changed. Thinking of others had not been one of those priorities. Life consisted of doing the next thing to move up the corporate ladder.

Mandi and el Padre walked over to an area where they could sit. They sat in silence for a few moments longer as they viewed the landscape. Mandi broke the silence, and they resumed talking where they left off. "It's fitting that we're talking about contrast. I guess that's really why I'm here," she said sort of matter-of-factly, still staring at the landscape.

"Not following you."

Thinking of her daily routine in her office and her constant connectedness to the electronic world, she elaborated. "Life can get so complicated."

"It's only complicated if you let it."

"Well, maybe so." Breaking her stare, Mandi looked at el Padre. "This is the first real break I've gotten from work where I've really gotten my mind off everything that relates to my life, and I feel so free. No blackberry. No laptop. No cell phone. No electronic leashes."

He looked at her and gently probed. "Kind of freeing, huh?"

She nodded with a smile. Taking a deep breath, she soaked it all up, getting a taste of peace as her cares of what she thought mattered slowly melted away. *This is why they have joy.* Mandi looked back at the horizon. "As a 'thirty-something,'" she said with air quotes, "I have accomplished great things at work. I have a great job. I make great money. I've climbed the corporate ladder quicker than any of my peers. But I still feel empty, like I'm missing something. How is it we get so wrapped up in life, so wrapped up in the daily grind, so wrapped up in ourselves we forget to look outside us and see what else is going on in the world?" Mandi was a little surprised at the words coming out of her mouth. She wondered where all this was coming from. She wondered what her mother would think. Too bad she couldn't come on this trip. She wished she could have made it.

The words were no surprise to el Padre, knowing exactly how Mandi was feeling. "There you go—another contrast." He paused. "When we start looking outside ourselves, we see a different world. Different things start to matter. Guatemala will do that to you. It's the simplicity here that makes it so attractive."

Mandi agreed. "It's like I'm getting a break"—she paused and added softly—"from me." A slight breeze blew over her, and she could smell the air, the dust, the trees, and the heat all at once. She took a deep breath and on the exhale felt her cares release.

"Wow. That was pretty quick."

She looked at him, puzzled.

"Most people don't feel that for a couple of days. And we're just at the start of your journey. I think this is going to be a great trip for you, Mandi."

"That's funny. My mom said the same thing, the great trip part."

He laughed. "So, what made you to decide to come on this trip?"

"My mom sort of talked me into it. She was actually going to come on the trip too. It was going to be a time for us to bond, but my dad fell off a ladder a couple weeks ago and has to go to therapy. It was a pretty bad fall—he punctured a lung, broke two ribs, and did something to his shoulder. The therapy is for his shoulder. Anyway, she was really disappointed she couldn't go but thought it would be better to stay back with dad and help him as he hobbles around."

El Padre nodded.

Mandi thought back for a moment, back to the phone conversation in which her mother had talked her into coming on this trip. She was between meetings and hadn't called in a while. After the conversational warm up of "How's everyone doing?" and "How's the dog?" the conversation eventually shifted to Mandi and her obsession with climbing the corporate ladder, and how there's more to life than money. Mandi started to tune her out. She looked on her desk where mounds of paperwork surrounded her. This hadn't been their first discussion on this topic. Mandi groaned to herself. Not this again, she thought.

"Hey, Mom, I'm going to need to run soon," she said. She could not grasp what her mother was talking about. Or she didn't want to—one of the two. Mandi knew her mother was proud of her and her successes, just the same as she was for her brother. But Mandi wondered why she needed to explain the "American dream" to her mother. Her mother, the most successful woman she

knew, had been the Dean of Science at the local university. As a woman in a man's field, she did pretty well for herself, thought Mandi. Why does she not see that's what I'm doing?

Her mother, now retired, was enjoying the next stage of life. She had money, prestige, and a beautiful home. She had it all: dinner parties, cocktail parties, corporate living. She'd been happily married for thirty-eight years, had two wonderful and self-sufficient grown children, and was looking forward to the day when she would be a grandmother, which, if left up to Mandi, would be awhile. What else could she possibly want? *She's got it all.*

Apparently, there was a lot that Mandi did not know, her mother explained. "Remember a few years ago, when I went to Central America? You had just finished college and were starting on your own path. You had just gotten your first promotion, just a month after starting your job."

"Yup, the first of many," Mandi responded, maybe a little too proudly.

Her mother dismissed it and continued: "On that trip, our university co-sponsored some local doctors to perform an experimental procedure for cleft-pallet repair where it would not be as invasive. It's something we'd been working on for a while."

"I remember. When you came back, that's all you could talk about." She was playing with her pen set on her desk, trying to spin it around her hand.

"That's right. That trip was my 'defining moment'—as a dean, as a scientist, as a woman, as a mother, as a person."

Mandi stopped playing with her pen. "Wasn't that also when you became a Christian?"

"Yes," said her mom. "It was the first time it was no longer about me. What we did mattered, Mandi. It was life changing. It was freeing. It gave meaning to everything. Seeing those children was heartbreaking, and I wanted more. I couldn't stop thinking about the children. I was burdened, saddened, *and alive with joy all at once. This might sound crazy, but I want that for you, Mandi. I think that is probably the greatest gift you could receive."*

"To be burdened, saddened, and alive with joy all at once?" Mandi asked.

"Yes, that's what will be your defining moment. I want that for you, Mandi. I want you to have your 'defining moment.' What do you think about going on a mission trip with me?" she asked. "Our church is going to build a house for a family in Guatemala. What do you think?"

"Defining moment" is a stretch, thought Mandi. But as she weighed it in her mind, Mandi thought it would be a chance to do a "good deed," something she hadn't done in years. And besides, going on the mission trip would offer a break from her crazy schedule, something she'd been needing for a while.

More thoughts weighed in Mandi's mind, and her reservations started to surface. Even though Mandi was open to the idea of going on a mission trip, the idea of hanging around a bunch of "Christians" wasn't high on her list. Her mom was a Christian, but it had been a pretty recent thing. Mandi hadn't grown up in church, and she didn't know what she would say to them.

"I'm not sure we'd have a lot in common," she told her mother, a little hesitantly.

Her mom laughed. "Don't be silly. They're like anybody else you would talk to. They're pretty normal," she added. Mandi could see her mother, even through the phone, nodding her head.

Mandi remembered the last time she was in a church. It was some time back in high school. She went a few times with her friend Julie, but that was so long ago. She remembered the people seemed nice, but because it didn't make any real connection and because her family did not go to church, she never went back.

"Do you remember Julie? She still goes there."

Julie was one of her better friends in high school, but Mandi wasn't very good at maintaining friendships, unless she needed to maintain it for personal gain. Mandi had seen her only a few times since high school, over fifteen years ago. They had a lot of fun in math class, she remembered. Julie liked to play pranks on Mandi and always caught her off guard. That was one of the things Mandi liked about her. Mandi laughed to herself, remembering when Julie somehow tied Mandi's shoe laces together. The bell rang for the end of math class, and as they got up to leave, Mandi took one step and fell into Josh Anderson, her "crush" in her junior year. It was not so funny at the time. But it did get her noticed and eventually, he asked her to the junior prom.

"How is she doing?" asked Mandi curiously.

"She's married and has two kids now," said her mom. "She asks about you every now and then. She's going on the trip."

"Really. That's cool." *Thinking it might be fun to reconnect, Mandi reconsidered.* "You know, that might be fun. Sign me up. I'll go."

Mandi heard a knock at the door to her office. Her assistant stepped in. "Next meeting starts in five." *Mandi nodded and her assistant left.*

"So, you'll go? That would be great. I'm so excited," said her mother. "I think this will be a great trip for you."

Mandi looked at el Padre. "So I told her I'd go and here I am."

"Well, I'm glad you're here. Your mom sounds like she's a pretty smart lady."

"Yeah, she is. She always amazes me. I don't always like what she says, but usually she's right. I hate that." She smiled. "I came on this trip for her. It was going to be our time together. She was going to show me my 'defining moment.'"

"Defining moment?"

"Oh, I don't know. It was something she talked about. You asked why I came on the trip. Really I just wanted to get a break from work, but I thought it would be nice to do a good deed."

"A good deed," he repeated. "That's a good start."

"What do you mean, 'a good start'?"

"You'll see." He got up and dusted off his pants. "My break is over. I'll see you later. I need to head back to the school now. Nice meeting you, Mandi." He looked her in the eyes. "I'm glad you're here."

Mandi smiled. She was glad she was here too.

"I'll be coming by again tomorrow, so, until then." Mandi lifted her camera to take a photo of el Padre walking away. He turned around and smiled. "My backside is not my best side."

"You're right!" Mandi laughed as he left, "See you tomorrow." Looking off into the horizon, Mandi sat there a little while longer to soak in the view and take a few more photos of the landscape before she got up and went back to the work site.

The boys took a break from the missing-wheel horse catapult game and watched curiously as they saw people doing various jobs. The site leader showed one of the team members how to look into the surveying scope to determine how to make sure the land was level. A group of people was leveling the last of the unfinished areas with picks to ensure the ground was ready for the cement slab. The team that assembled formers, long two-by-four boards assembled in a sixteen-foot rectangle, hammered long metal rods into the ground to hold the former in place. Extra rods were driven in to keep them from moving out once the cement was poured. A couple of men read the instruction manual in order to assemble the cement mixers.

Julie and Mandi looked at each other.

Mandi said matter-of-factly, "Engineers?"

Julie laughed. "You're right."

They all heard the honk of the delivery truck at the bottom of the hill. The site leader got everyone's attention. "Hey guys, looks like the cement was just delivered. It's at the bottom of the hill. There are about thirty-three bags, and they weigh over ninety pounds each. Team up if you have to, but be careful because the hill is steep, and the path is a bit slippery."

Everyone took a break from their jobs and headed down the hill to grab the bags of cement. Mandi and her friend Julie paired up. "This is not as easy as I thought it would be," said Mandi, huffing about a third of the way up the hill.

"This is not easy at all," replied Julie, struggling to maintain the hold.

Boy carrying cement up the hill. It was amazing to see them. The boy's father brought up two cement bags at one time, one similarly susspended from his head and the other on his back.

They didn't get very far when the father and the oldest son, Roberto, came to help. Using hand gestures, they offered to take their cement bag. Roberto hoisted the cement bag over his shoulders while the father went down and got a bag. Mandi and Julie waited to catch their breath, grateful they didn't have to bring it up the rest of the way.

At the next trip, the father brought up two bags at one time.

Apparently, he was much stronger than his five-foot-two frame looked. He supported a sling tied to a strap and placed it near his forehead. The second bag was perched crosswise on top of the other bag.

"Do you see that?" asked Mandi incredulously.

"Yeah," said Julie, "those two bags weigh more than he does!"

"How can he carry all that? Together, we couldn't even carry one!"

Julie shook her head in disbelief.

Feeling a bit humbled, they headed back up the hill, marveling at how strong the men were and how hard they worked. "Wish I would have brought my camera down," said Mandi from the steep incline between breaths. "No one's going to believe that one!"

With the cement here and everything ready with the foundation, the cement party was about to begin. Everyone picked a station as the hum of the rotating cement mixers filled the air. As people manned their stations, they lined up five-gallon buckets of water, rock, sand, and mortar behind the two electric cement mixers. The cement recipe called for buckets, three-quarters full, of rock, sand, water, mortar, rock, sand, rock, sand. That was the order. They made a song of

Members of the team loading up the cement mixer.

it, similar to the song from the rock band Police. "Rock-sand" instead of Roxanne.

Mandi used unfamiliar muscles, muscles that had probably never ever been used. The work was hard, but it felt good. Mandi noticed how her cares from work and home were slowly disappearing, melting from her mind. The smell of sunscreen permeated the area as the sun baked their ears, necks, and noses. Sweat poured off their bodies. Mandi felt the salt from her sweat stick to her clothes. When the family brought a watermelon at midday, it was a glorious, welcomed break from the hard work. The father set a papaya and a watermelon on the pink children's table. Next to it, he set down his aged, dull machete. The team graciously accepted the offer and determined it was some of the best fruit they had ever tasted. The team shared candy that they brought with the kids in the area, and Mandi took more photos. She took photos of the team interacting with the nearby families, who watched with curiosity as their neighbor's house was being built by strangers.

Capturing candid moments with her camera, Mandi wondered what they thought. *What do they think of their neighbors getting a new home? How do they feel? Are they happy for them? Does this team offer these people hope—the hope that maybe they could be next?* Mandi was shaken out of her thoughts as Carlos squealed down the hill on that crazy toy horse then went midair. Chuckling to herself, she got back to work.

Rock, sand, water, mortar, rock, sand, rock, sand. The cement was mixed and dumped over and over again. Eventually, the forms were full, and two men smoothed out the top of the cement, completing the foundation. It was a long day, and Mandi could already feel bruises forming on her forearms from lifting the heavy buckets to the cement mixer. The sun and oxygen at this altitude tired her more than she thought they would. Once the buckets, tools, and cement mixers were clean, the site leader gathered everyone around the area again, and together they thanked God for the productive day and prayed for the homeowners. Again, the boys watched on, as did the neighboring Kristal and Javier. The team said good-bye and headed back down the steep incline to catch the bus. Completely exhausted yet nearly giddy, Mandi thought to herself, *What a long, hard, completely awesome day.* Carlos and Pedro waved to her as she left. She smiled and waved back, took her seat on the bus next to Julie, and smiled to herself.

5

SHOOTING STARS

Javier sat next to Mamá. "Tell me another story," he says, listening to her every word. His favorite one Mamá tells is when she got her first pair of shoes. She said she could run as fast as a shooting star.

"Javi, I was your age when I got my first pair of shoes. You are a lucky boy because you already have shoes."

He looked at his feet and saw his two shoes that did not match. Tío had tied a block under Javier's left foot, so his legs would be the same length. His left leg was not only shorter, but weaker too. Because of this, he needed two different sizes of shoes. Consequently, his shoes never matched, and often his right shoe was worn down so much that very little was holding it together.

"You are right, Mamá. I am lucky." Javier's left leg was not very strong, but he hoped that someday, he would like to be like his Mamá and be as fast as a shooting star.

While Mamá was talking, Tío bundled up the firecracker wicks. "I am going to the fireworks factory, Javi. Want to come with me?" He hoisted the bundle on his back.

Javier dropped the wick he was working on and jumped up excitedly. "¡Sí!" he exclaimed in agreement.

As they walked, Javier told Tío the story his Mamá had told him about shoes and shooting stars.

"I remember when she got those shoes," said Tío, thinking back to when he and his sister were younger. "She was like lightning, Javi. She was very fast, fast like a shooting star bolting across the sky. You will not believe this, but she was even faster than me!"

"Faster than you?" Javier said, unbelievingly. He tried to picture his mother healthy, but since he had never seen that (he had only seen her cough), it seemed like another story.

"It is true. Did you know, Javi, that when you see a shooting star, you are supposed to make a wish?"

"I will remember that." Javier smiled. "The next time I see a shooting star, I will wish for strong legs. And I will be lightning fast, just like Mamá."

"That is a good wish. Dreams are free, Javi. Dream big." They continued their walk to the pueblo and passed some of the girls who were carrying drinking water back from the well and greeted them. "Your Mamá is right, Javi," said Tío. "You are a lucky boy. You are not like all the other boys. You have many other strengths that they do not have"— Javier looked at him inquisitively, as if to ask, like what?—"strengths like you know how many newspaper strips we will need to make a bundle of wicks. You know when to stop so it will not be too heavy for me to carry. You know how much corn we need for tortillas and when we will need to barter for more. You know when it will rain so Rodrigo wears the right clothes when he goes out to the fields. You know many things, Javi. Many things that boys your age do not know. You are perceptive. Very perceptive. You know what people are thinking."

Things just naturally came to Javier; he didn't have to think about it. He just naturally assumed everyone was like that.

"Not everyone can do things you can do. You may not be strong in your leg, but you are very strong in your mind," Tío continued.

Javier thought for a second. He never realized that.

"You make us very proud, Javi."

Javi held himself a little taller on their walk.

As they walked and talked, the fireworks factory seemed to suddenly appear. "We got here very fast," said Javier, surprised it was so soon.

Tío smiled and tousled Javier's hair. "Wait here. I will be right back."

Children were not allowed inside. Tío would be only a few minutes, so Javier waited outside the building. To pass the time, Javier eyed a medium-sized rock just off to the side. *Perfect for target practice.* As Javier bent down to pick up some smaller stones to throw, he saw an intense flash of light, followed by a thunderous, deafening noise. He felt instant heat and pain, and then just as suddenly, did not see or feel or hear anything. Nothing.

The loud explosion resonated around the mountainside and echoed in the valley. Noise and brilliant lights and chaos surrounded the factory. Like ants scurrying when their mound was disturbed, people flowed from all directions.

Javier's body was launched into the air from the explosion as displays of fireworks suddenly lit up the sky. Brilliant colors and lights shot across the sky, like shooting stars. Javier landed several feet away, unconscious.

Fireworks shot off in all directions, and everyone knew what had just happened. Women watched, frozen and unable to move, terrified that this was a repeat from two years ago that had killed eight people in the pueblo. It looked just like the last explosion: people running around, people being dragged out, dark smoke billowing in the air, fireworks exploding above all the smoke—it all looked the same.

After the last explosion, they had placed some regulations on the factory, like no smoking in the building. At first the rules were strongly adhered to, but eventually people went back to their same routine. They still smoked in their offices, but not near the fireworks area. The only rule that was really completely adhered to was they no longer allowed children inside. The owner's son had been killed, along with two other children, in the last explosion. Since then, no child had entered the building.

Slowly, blurry images faded in and out of Javier's view as his eyes adjusted to the noise and commotion. A man hovered over him. He could tell the man was yelling something at him, but his mind was like a vacuum, and he couldn't hear a word. Javier could see fireworks shooting up over his head. *Is that a shooting star?* he thought through the haze. *What did Tío say I need to do when I see a shooting star?*

Javier stared at the man, confused, not understanding a word, unable to process. He blinked. Noise and confusion was everywhere. The ringing in his ears was intense. He closed his eyes for a few seconds, a long deliberate blink. When he reopened them, the ringing became a loud, muffled, slow-motion echo. He could not think in sentences. Explosion. Noise. Fireworks. People. Running. The man was still yelling at him. *Why is he so excited? Why is everything in slow motion? Why does it sound like I am inside a bucket?* He blinked again, slowly and deliberately. On the third time he blinked, he pieced it together. His thoughts finally caught up with the commotion surrounding him. "Oh no!" he said, regaining his senses. He tried to leap up, but his movements were slow and unstable. "My Tío!" yelled Javier. "Tío is inside! My Tío is inside!"

"Hold still, Javier. You may be hurt," said the man that hovered over him. Javier recognized him, but his mind was still cloudy. With his limited hearing, he picked out a few words. "Hold. Still. Hurt." His thoughts were slow. "Javier, are you OK?"

"Me? I am fine." The ringing intensified.

"You do not look fine," said the man. "You should lay down until we find help."

"I am fine," Javier said again. "Where is Tío?" Javier asked, frantic. He tried to get back on his feet but was unsuccessful. He looked around for Tío, but could not see him through the flurry of people and noise and confusion. Nearby, people from the pueblo rushed to tend to the injured.

Focusing his attention on the man who was hovering over him, Javier was able to piece the words together. The man was yelling, "Your Tío is hurt. We will take care of him here. Are you sure you are OK?"

Javier slowly got up, still a little confused and dizzy. He patted his arms and legs and chest to see that everything was still there. "I think so," said Javier, more as a question than a statement. He touched his ears and head and felt something sticky. He looked at his hands. It was blood. He felt a bump on his head and realized that was where the blood was coming from. He still felt ringing in his ears, but he felt like his balance was returning. He looked at the man. He said yes and slowly nodded his head. "I think I am OK."

It was enough to convince the man. "Then you must run. Run and get your Tía!"

Javier tried to balance himself and rested his arm on the man's shoulder; his knees wobbled.

The man helped hold him up. Then he gave Javier a good pat on the back. "Go, Javier! Go get your Tía!"

Javier nodded and tried to move, tried to run, but the dizziness and ringing in his ears froze him in place. He willed his legs to move. Eventually, they started moving forward, slowly at first, then building up to a full hobble. He moved as fast as his deformed leg could take him, across the wreckage and rocks. In the explosion, he had lost his shoes and the wooden block for his foot, so the unevenness of his legs further complicated his balance. He concentrated his footing across the rutty, pot-holed road that took them to their casa. The muscles in his legs were clenching in pain, and he could feel his head pounding, about to explode in his mind with every heartbeat. He could feel burning in his bad leg as he ran. *Just about there,* he convinced himself. Recognizing landmarks as he got closer to home, he forced himself to keep moving. The ringing in his ears battled for his attention. *Must. Keep. Moving. Almost. Home.* Suddenly, shards of pain shot through his leg and up his back, followed by intense brightness. Then, just as suddenly, complete darkness. His body hit the hard ground.

The explosion was heard by everyone in the pueblo and could be felt for miles around. Rodrigo was listening intently to el Padre talk about a place called the United States. "The United States has many states," explained el Padre. "The state I am from is called Tennessee. Tennessee has mountains like here in Guatemala." The noise boomed over el Padre's lecture. Students felt the vibration of the explosion course through their body, suddenly jolted from their chairs, their minds brought back to their classroom in Guatemala. Rodrigo looked up and saw smoke billowing. They all knew it was the fireworks factory. Rodrigo knew that if anyone was hurt, he would know them. A knot formed in his stomach. *Who would it be?* he thought nervously.

El Padre looked up and saw the billowing smoke and said a prayer for those involved. "God, be with us today. Please help us. Help the injured and heal them. Lord, we put the healing in your hands."

No one in the class moved for a few seconds. They felt the shock-waves and were frozen in their chairs.

Kristal and Marissa arrived with their water jugs still on their heads, and they ran to see if anyone was hurt. As they got closer to the factory, people were running around frantically trying to help. Others were pulling workers out of the factory on whatever make-shift stretchers they could find. Whatever could be found—old doors, boards—was used to pull out the injured. Another crowd started to form—wives of the workers. Women ran around the scene, looking for their husbands. Screams and crying and chaos filled the air.

Kristal looked down and saw several men in her pueblo that she knew who worked there. *Who is still inside?* she wondered frantically.

Marissa was paralyzed in place, recounting the scene from two years ago. Men and children had been scattered about the area with charred shirts. Screaming and crying had filled the air as fireworks lit the sky. Marissa saw it all again. The images of two years ago replayed in her mind: the chaos and confusion; the men huddled over a body; the looks on their faces as they saw Marissa and her mother walking closer to the body; the look of the man who told them the bad news; the look on her mother's face when she heard the bad news; and the body of her father. Marissa's father had been one of the eight that did not survive.

"Marissa! They need our help!" yelled Kristal.

Marissa stood there, trying to shake the scene from her memory, but it was almost exactly the same. The same chaos and smoke and screaming.

"Marissa!" Kristal shook Marissa to pull her out of her frozen thoughts. It was no use, realized Kristal, and she walked briskly towards the men with her water vessel still on her head.

Men were gathered in a circle, tending to someone in the middle. She grabbed the water vessel and lowered it down to the ground. Kristal saw confusion and pain everywhere around her. She was concerned, concerned she would know who was inside, worried about who was injured, and worse yet, who was—Kristal did not allow herself to complete that thought. Her mind snapped back to the situation at hand.

She grabbed her shawl and dipped it in the vessel and walked toward the men gathered in a circle. They were hovering over someone. A man with a charred shirt and soot-covered face looked up and recognized Kristal. He got up and with a faint limp started walking towards Kristal, grabbing his leg as he walked. He winced but kept getting closer. Just then the men moved, and Kristal saw who they were hovering over. Her heart sank. It was Tío. His shirt was torn and smoldered. She saw blackened, sooty skin and blood and saw he was not moving. The man with the injured leg was close enough to yell out, "Your Tío is hurt very badly. We do not know if he will survive. Javi has already left to go tell your Tía. I do not know how fast he can run. He was hurt too."

"Tío!" she repeated in disbelief, as she bent down to touch his face. Her heart raced in panic as she saw her uncle lying there. "Tío! Tío!" she yelled. His eyes opened slightly but he did not move. Kristal bent over his body. His breathing was shallow, and he had many cuts over his face. She put the shawl on him to wipe away some of the blood and started to cry.

The man with the limp bent down and looked her in the eyes. He repeated what he said earlier. "Javi has already left to go tell your Tía. He was hurt too."

"Javi? Javi was hurt too? He left to tell Tía?" asked Kristal. The words finally lined up in her mind for her to understand. She gave the shawl she was using to wipe down Tío's face to the man who spoke to her and ran like she had never run before.

Trees and bushes blurred as Kristal focused her attention on what was in front of her. All she heard was her footsteps hitting the hard ground, occasional branches snapping, and her steady breathing in and out. On the road, she made an effort to avoid the ruts, the ravines, and the stray chickens. Almost home, near the foot of the last hill, she saw something laying on the ground. As she got closer, she realized it was Javier, limp and unconscious. She bent down.

"Oh no! Javi! Javi! Wake up! Are you OK?" She screamed and shook him. "Javi! Wake up!"

Javier's eyes blinked a few times. Someone was shouting at him. More ringing in his years. He tried to focus on the face. He recognized it. It was hard for one thought to connect to the next thought. "Wake up!" he heard again. He saw lips moving. He thought he knew who it was. *What is she saying?*, he wondered. His mind was trying to catch up, but time and thoughts moved very slowly and did not connect to-gether. He blinked several times then realized it was Kristal.

"Javi, are you OK?"

"Kristal!" He tried hard to forms words. It was so difficult. Everything echoed in his head. "Tío . . . explosion . . . factory. Needs help!"

"I know! We must tell Tía!"

"I tried, Kristal." His body started to tremble, followed up with sobs. "I tried."

"Come on, Javi." She took his face in her hands so he could see and hear her. "You were very brave, Javi. We need to get you home. Are you ready?" Her mind was screaming. "We've got to go! We need to get help for Tío!"

"Yes, I am ready," he whispered.

"OK, this might hurt a little. Let's go." Kristal tried to carry Javier up the hill to the house, but even as strong as she was, the best she could do was drag him. Javier winced in pain.

Tía had been preparing tortillas for lunch. Her hands were covered in masa. Mamá was cutting tomatoes. Tía and Mamá saw Kristal dragging Javier up the hill, his limp body being pulled up. They ran towards Kristal. "Kristal, what happened?" asked Mamá as she reached down to help with Javi. They helped Kristal ease him down to the ground.

"Mamá, it was awful," said Kristal, moving so Javier could get comfortable. Tía had the quick realization that Javier wouldn't be anywhere without Tío. "Tío! Where is Tío?" asked Tía, nervously.

Still out of breath, Kristal blurted, "Something terrible has happened to Tío! He was at the factory when it exploded. He is hurt!"

Tía immediately had a look of panic as she ran in the direction of the factory.

"Javi, tell me what happened," said Mamá, fearfully.

Javier had never heard that tone in her voice before. He was confused and in pain, and somewhere Tío needed some help. Words were painfully difficult to form, and as hard as he tried, he could not find any to say. *How did I get here? Where is Tío?* That's what he wanted to ask. He fought to stay awake, but he was slowly losing that battle. Javier did not know how he had gotten here. In his mother's arms, Javier looked up and in a haze, he saw remnants of fireworks shower the air looking much like shooting stars. Then he drifted off.

"Javi!" yelled Mamá, shaking him awake. "Tell me what happened," Mamá repeated.

Javier tried again to focus, but it all felt like a dream. And as hard as he tried, he could not get out of it. Mamá held him tight and started rocking them on the ground. Tears started to flow down her cheeks. Javier started to remember odd thoughts. *Why is the fireworks factory painted red? Why was everyone running around? What are shooting stars made out of?* Then he heard Tío whisper in his mind, *"When you see a shooting star, make a wish."*

"Tío? Where are you?" he tried to ask, but the words were not very audible. He was succumbing to confusion and sleep. *I . . . will not . . . wish . . . for strong legs today.* Javier closed his eyes and whispered, "I wish . . . for Tío . . . to be well." He then drifted off to sleep again, this time resting in Mamá's arms.

The smell of burnt tortillas filled the air. Kristal, weak-kneed from running, hobbled over to remove them from the flat tin that they were being cooked on, burning her fingers as she pulled them off. She pushed the flat tin that was used for cooking tortillas on from the fire, careful not to touch it too long with her fingers so she wouldn't get burnt from that too. It fell to the ground. Too tired and weak to move anymore, she just left it there. She wiped some sweat from her forehead and realized she had blood on her arms. *I will get that off later.*

Mamá held Javier and gently rocked him, and they all silently prayed for Tío.

6

WHEN THE SUN BROKE THROUGH

The words of Marissa kept haunting Kristal: "If you do not have hope, you have nothing. That is what el Padre says." Kristal tried to console Rodrigo with those words, but as she put her hand on his shoulder, he pushed it away. Upset that he would have to quit school, upset that at age twelve, he was now the man of the house, he kicked the ground.

"Those words mean nothing. What is hope? We have no hope," he said despairingly. "We have nothing. Why us?" He paused and added hopelessly, "Why me?"

"It is only until Tío gets well," offered Javier, trying to be optimistic.

"I will never get to go to school! I will never be able to read or get a smart person's job!" Nearly in tears and feeling defeated, Rodrigo despairingly added in a soft tone, "And worse, I will never be able to provide Mamá a home."

"It will be OK, Rodrigo," said Javier, still sore from the explosion two days ago.

Kristal patted his shoulder. "We will think of something." Her attempt at optimism was weak, but she tried to console Rodrigo.

The three of them sat by the edge of their plot and looked down at the house being built by the missionaries. The framework was up now, and it was starting to look like a home. A fire was burning on the stove while the family huddled around talking.

Rodrigo took a deep breath. "Why can't that be us?" Anger was building up in his voice. "Mamá is sick, Tío is hurt, and I can't go to school to learn to read!" His anger mounted. With a clenched fist, he hit the palm of his other hand and yelled out, "Why? Why God? Why won't you help us?"

They sat in silence for a while, then very softly, Javier said something. Rodrigo could not hear as all his angry thoughts were in the way. But Kristal heard it. Her eyes darted over to Javier, piercing him with her glare. Rodrigo saw her glare, and was confused. He cocked his head to the side wondering, *what did Javier just say?* Then, as if the clouds were removed and the sun broke through, Rodrigo understood it all and he smiled. His anger completely gone, he nodded his head in approval and said, "Javi, I am glad you are the optimist!" Then Rodrigo looked intently at his sister and continued, "Kristal, I am the new man of the house now until Tío is well enough."

She did not like how this conversation was going.

"One of us must go to school so we can change the way we live." He gently reached out for her arm. "It must be you. You must be our hope"

When he said it like that, she knew that no was not an option. This was way too important for Rodrigo to compromise on. Too important for any of them to compromise on, she realized, and her heart sank. In a low voice, she told him, "Because you are the man of the house for

now, I will do this. I will do this for you and for Mamá and our family
. . . for now."

Rodrigo winked at Javier, pleased with their plan. Javier smiled
back at him and he and Kristal went inside. They looked at Rodrigo.
"Are you coming in?"

"I'll be right back," he said. "I have a small errand I need to do."
Rodrigo wanted Kristal to be ready to start school in the morning, so he
went to Marissa's family's house to barter a uniform skirt. He figured
his white button-down shirt from his uniform should fit her pretty
well and made sure it was clean. Everything was ready. He waited until
the next morning to give the uniform to his sister, just in case she had
plans to hide them.

Mamá had a difficult night of coughing and trying to catch her
breath, so they all wanted her to rest. She tried to get up earlier but just
didn't have the energy to make breakfast. Kristal told her to go back to
bed. "I will make breakfast, Mamá."

Mamá squeezed her hand. "Thank you, sweet girl."

Kristal liked it when her mother called her that.

Rodrigo was outside, starting the fire. "I'd like to get an early start,"
he said. "I'd like to get going right after breakfast, OK?"

Kristal nodded her head. She started to prepare the coffee and
make masa for tortillas.

"Oh, and here," he said, "try this on." He pulled her arms out so she
would take the clothes.

She recognized them. It was her new school uniform. She took the
clothes and finished making breakfast.

A few minutes later she hesitantly returned with the uniform on.
"It's a little big but mostly fits," she reported.

Still holding a tortilla, Rodrigo said, encouragingly, "I think it looks great."

Javier was sitting on a stump near the fire and looked up. "You look very smart today. I think you will have a good day."

Rodrigo smiled at him as if to say thanks for encouraging her.

She forced a smile, still reluctant to go. She did not understand this hope he talked about and wasn't sure she really wanted to. "I will go," she said despairingly, "but I do not think it will be a good day."

"Be like Javi." Rodrigo reached out and put his hand on her shoulder. "Be optimistic."

She brushed it off. "I am not optimistic, and I am not happy."

She was about to stomp out of the area when Rodrigo said, "Say good-bye to Mamá. It's time to go."

Kristal peeked in and patted Mamá's hand, stirring her. She looked so tiny under her Mayan blanket. "Mamá," she said softly. "We are getting ready to go." Kristal bent down to give Mamá a kiss. Kristal could see Tío inside also. She saw bandages all over his face and upper body, Mamá looked up and said weakly, "Be smart, sweet girl," and she squeezed Kristal's hand.

"Yes, Mamá." Kristal smiled and left the room.

Rodrigo walked her there the first day even though she knew the way to the school. He wanted to make sure she would find it and help her settle in, he told her, but really he wanted to make sure she would go. He was still not convinced she would actually go. As they talked along the way, Rodrigo told her about some of the other students in his class, about the teachers, and what to expect. "You will like el Padre. And Ms. Sharon is very nice too. She has a pet parrot she sometimes brings to class."

They walked up to the gate. Kristal took a deep breath, and Rodrigo met her eyes with a look that said it was going to be okay. Ms. Sharon was the first to greet them. She immediately let them in. "You must be Kristal. I've heard a lot about you," Ms. Sharon said, warmly.

Kristal looked at Rodrigo. *What did you tell her?* she wondered.

Ms. Sharon asked about Mamá and Tío. "How are they doing? Are they feeling better?"

While Ms. Sharon and Kristal were getting to know each other, Rodrigo spoke with el Padre off to the side. "No, she did not want to come," he explained.

El Padre nodded at him reassuringly. He put his hand on Rodrigo's shoulder. "I am sure you are confused and angry as to why all this has happened. And while I know it is you who would like to be here instead of your sister, I have to believe there is a reason things are working out this way."

Rodrigo nodded acceptingly. "I hope to be back as soon as Tío gets better. Until then, I have to be man of the house."

"You are being very grown up right now, Rodrigo. I'm proud of you. We always say around here that the Lord works in mysterious ways. Trust Him. I know that's not always that easy, but that's a hard lesson in faith." Rodrigo nodded again, and gave him a faint smile. Behind el Padre, Rodrigo saw Ms. Sharon's parrot and his smile got bigger.

"Perfect." Rodrigo smiled. *Kristal will love her parrot,* he thought. "OK, I must go." He had firecracker wicks to roll that day. Lots of them, as he was not as fast as Tío.

Before Rodrigo left, el Padre shook his hand. "We'll take care of her, Rodrigo." He knew they would. He just wondered how Kristal would take all this. Hope was not something she held to tightly; as the oldest in the family and the one most focused on daily living and next meals, she was very good at making sure the family's needs were met. Kristal did not have time for lofty thoughts like hope and things like that. Rodrigo smiled at her as he left and felt at peace about this. *It's going to be OK,* he thought. He was pretty sure Kristal was not thinking the same thing, but hoped she would still like it. School was something he already missed even though it had only been a few days since he had last attended.

Kristal looked back at Rodrigo and returned his look with a slight smile as he walked out of the door. At age thirteen, Kristal was starting first grade.

El Padre told Ms. Sharon they would be right back. "I am going to show Kristal around the school. We will be back in a little bit." He walked her around the school, explaining what was in each building. Kristal had not yet spoken, but when she walked into the large building, her reaction was much the same as Rodrigo's. With eyes wide open, she took everything in.

El Padre watched as her reluctance faded. *It's going to be OK.*

She noticed the concrete floor, the large room, and rooms off to the side. "What is that room?" she asked curiously, uttering her first words spoken at the school. The "office" that doubled as the doctor's office, administration office, and library was the most interesting thing she'd ever seen.

"Let's go look," said el Padre. "Do you like books?"

Kristal nodded.

"I should have guessed so. Rodrigo loved them too."

They walked into the room. She eyed the books, the large desk for the administrator, and off to the side, the other area that the doctor used. His examining table was on the far side. On the countertop were some of the doctor's instruments. She saw a long curtain that could be pulled across the room to close off the doctor's side from the school administration's side when the doctor needed to examine a patient. Kristal saw a jar full of wooden sticks and remembered the doctor used them to stick in peoples' mouths. She had seen a doctor only once, when she was around seven. She had been very sick. Kristal had spiked a very high fever, and Mamá was not able to get it to come down. At the fireworks plant, Tío had heard of a mission team that was doing dental work nearby. Tío carried her there to see if they could help. The doctor used one of those sticks to see the back of her throat and gave her a shot. Like magic, her fever broke, and she started to feel better. That place was set up sort of like this, she remembered.

El Padre let her look around a little and could tell she was now starting to get interested. He explained more information about the school. "The Christian school goes from kindergarten to sixth grade. We are hoping to expand into higher grades if it is 'God's will.'"

God's will, she understood, was another way of saying "funding permitting."

He continued, "The school exists solely on hope and donations. But so far, God has provided us what we need. I think He will want us to stay here a lot longer," said el Padre, "but that is up to Him."

As Kristal looked around, she guessed hope was working out for these people. El Padre looked at Kristal. "We are glad you are here, Kristal. I believe God has sent you here for a purpose. I want you to think about what that purpose is."

God sent me here for a purpose? It wasn't God—it was Rodrigo. Rodrigo sent me. He made me come here. She knew this to be true but did not say anything.

"We have miracles here, Kristal. In fact," he said with a bit of a laugh, "every month is a miracle." They walked closer to the shelves. "One month, we did not have enough money to pay the teachers. I was in despair. I was sad that we would not be able to pay them; they work so hard, and I was wondering why God did not provide. I am sad to say that on that day, the staff had more faith than me. They prayed for a miracle. They prayed they would have money to keep the school running." He looked at Kristal. "Do you know what happened?"

She shook her head no, but she was interested. She felt her heart softening as she listened.

He continued with excitement in his voice. "While the staff was praying—that very minute—a donation came in for the *exact* amount we needed to pay the teachers. Just like that." He shook his head in disbelief. *"The exact amount!* Who would know that we would have needed that certain amount? Only God would know that, Kristal. He did provide. It is all God, Kristal. He makes miracles all the time, but sometimes we don't recognize it."

Kristal felt a little overwhelmed. She did not expect all this on her first day of school.

El Padre said again that he thought Kristal was here for a reason. "You must find out why, Kristal. We are all here for a reason." They walked back into the large room, and Kristal looked around. "Do you know why I am here?" he asked, and again she shook her head no. "God told me to come here. He told me to come here to teach kids that look like you."

Kristal looked at him. As they walked out of the large building, towards one of the smaller single buildings, she made a mental inventory of "looks." El Padre was the first person Kristal had met that didn't have brown eyes. They were green. And his skin was very white, just like the people who come to build houses. And his short, wavy red hair was such a contrast to her long, black hair. He looked different, but it wasn't just his skin or his hair or his eyes. It took her a few moments to figure it out. Then she realized what it was that made him different. He had a certain happiness to him. Kristal looked at him and questioned, "God? God told you to come here? How did God do that? You cannot see Him or hear Him. How did He do that?"

"Well, it was in my head. It was a thought that God put there. I was being obedient to His command."

Not really sure what that meant, she listened.

"Who is your best friend, Kristal?" he asked.

"Marissa."

"So, why is she your best friend?"

Kristal never really thought about it before. "Because we talk and enjoy each other's company?" She was looking for affirmation.

He nodded at her response. "That's a good answer. And when you ask her if you should do something, do you usually listen?"

"Yes, usually."

"Well, that's how it is with God. He is my best friend, and He finds ways to communicate with us. Sometimes it's a feeling. Sometimes I really feel that I hear what He says. It's inside my head. In any case, that's how God communicates with me. So, when I got here, I came to teach for a little while, but when I thought it was time to go, God did not think so. I felt He wanted me to stay here longer. So, I stayed, and here I am."

El Padre had just completed his thought as they arrived in front of her classroom. "Well, here you go. I will stop by after class to see how it all went today." He opened the door for her. "Good luck!" he added, smiling, and left towards the big building to the office area.

Kristal took a deep breath as she walked in. Ms. Sharon introduced her to the class. "Class, this is Kristal, Rodrigo's older sister." They said hi. They all knew who she was. They all knew what had happened to her family. They all knew what had happened to the other families too and for a couple of days, no one really knew what to say to those affected. For those not immediately affected, school resumed as usual, but for those who had loved ones and friends involved, the struggle to get past the explosion was a little trickier. In all, there were two deaths from the recent fireworks explosion. Six more were injured badly, with Tío being one of the six. Everyone else, luckily, was fine. But the explosion emotionally scarred many people in the town.

Kristal's family had lots of people visit just after the explosion. Even el Padre stopped in. Tío was awake for some of the visitors, but Javier was awake for all of them. Javier enjoyed their company. One time, Javier explained to one of the visitors that in the explosion he learned how to fly in the air. "I just wasn't prepared for the landing," he said. For some reason, Javier started laughing, slowly at first, then a full-up belly laugh. He slowed down to catch his breath, then started giggling again. Through giggles, he said, "My arms made bad wings!" and he laughed harder. It was infectious and everyone laughed.

The laughter woke Tío, upsetting Tía. "Shhh. We need to let Tío rest so he can get strong again."

Tío brushed it off, waving his bandaged arm in the air. "Anytime my family is laughing, I want to be part of that," he said. With all of his bandages on, he could not see, but he could hear every bit of it from his good ear. Tía did not say any more about that. In fact, she joined in on the laughing too and realized laughter was the best healing they could have. It helped everyone to not feel the pain.

In the classroom, Kristal settled into her desk and learned about letters and sounds, just like Rodrigo explained it when he first went. She met Ms. Sharon's parrot, named Loco. Ms. Sharon spoke to it and asked, "What do you say to Kristal?" The class watched on from their seats, inquisitively.

"Hey, pretty girl," squawked Loco. Kristal put her hands over her mouth in astonishment.

"Rodrigo never told me that your parrot could speak!"

"He doesn't know. She just started doing it. I've tried to train her for years, then all of a sudden, she just starts talking. Crazy thing. Guess she is living up to her name!" The class laughed knowing that loco means crazy. The parrot had visited class for the last three years, and not once did it talk. This was the first time anyone had seen the parrot speak.

"Does Loco say anything else?" asked one of the students.

"Yes, at home. But I do not want to provoke her," said Ms. Sharon.

"Why? What does she say?" asked the same student, now curious.

Ms. Sharon reluctantly said, "OK, watch." She put her parrot on her arm and said, "What happened there, Loco?"

The parrot responded, "Uh oh. Made a mess." The class burst out in laughter. Loco was bobbing her head up and down, seemingly liking the attention. "Quiet please," she squawked. And the class laughed again.

"Wow," said Ms. Sharon. "Loco is having a great time today."

"I love you," it said and flew back to its perch on Ms. Sharon's desk, apparently done with the show.

"Well, you all had a real treat today. Loco has not performed like this ever before." Looking at her watch, she said, "Oh my, time has gotten away from us this morning. It is already time for lunch." Students who had lunches gathered up their bags to leave to go to the large room. Some students left to go home to eat, but others, especially those who did not bring a lunch, stayed at the school for lunch. Kristal thought about going home at lunchtime but knew the reality was that there was no extra food there.

"I will wait in the classroom while everyone eats," explained Kristal to Ms. Sharon. Kristal had not brought a lunch, or more correctly, did not have a lunch to bring. Now that Tío was not working, it was a little more difficult to get food. She did not have any extra to bring with her that day.

"You're coming with us," said Ms. Sharon, matter-of-factly, and they all walked down to the large room, which at this time of day would be called the lunchroom. Ms. Sharon led Kristal to the kitchen area, along with the other students who had not brought lunches, and they lined up. At the end of the line, there was a person giving students chewable vitamins. When they got to the food area, there was a very large silver pot full of something white and soupy looking. Kristal had not seen this food before.

"This is mash," explained Ms. Sharon. "The school provides it for students who do not have lunches. Here." She motioned to Kristal. "Take this bowl."

Kristal took the bowl and sat down with her class at one of the long tables. Kristal looked at the bowl in front of her, at the opaque white mixture, and tasted it. It was sweet. "How is it?" asked Ms. Sharon.

"I like it," said Kristal, though she would have told Ms. Sharon she liked it whether or not she really did. But she did like it. It had a soupy, watery consistency, with little grains of something, like corn.

"I thought you would," said Ms. Sharon, approvingly. Kristal ate a few bites, then stopped eating. She could taste something else but wasn't sure what it was. She guessed it was the vitamins. All she knew was it wasn't too bad for her first taste of mash. Getting lost in her thoughts, she recounted her day. *This is not at all how I thought my first day of school would be like. Why would I not want to come here?* She thought of Rodrigo, sad for him that he could not be here. She thought of Javi. *Javi would be happy that I am being optimistic. Well, mostly optimistic.* She smiled to herself.

Ms. Sharon looked at Kristal. "Are you OK?" she asked.

"Yes," said Kristal, bringing her thoughts back to the lunchroom. "I am good," she said, and meant it.

At the end of the day, el Padre came in to check up on her, just like he said he would. The students had all left, and he took a seat on the long bench across from her. Her friend Marissa waited outside. Kristal smiled as he came in.

"How was your first day?" he asked.

"It was very good. Much better than I expected. Ms. Sharon's parrot was funny."

"I heard Loco put on quite a show. Must have been for you," he said as Kristal nodded. "Did you think any more on why God brought you here?"

Kristal stopped nodding her head and looked at him, still unsure of her answer.

"There is a verse in the Bible in the book of John, where Jesus says, 'You did not choose me, but I chose you and appointed you so that you might go and bear fruit—fruit that will last—and so that whatever you ask in my name the Father will give you.' When you have Jesus in your heart, you have everything. That, Kristal, is hope. Hope you can trust in."

She started to understand a different kind of hope, not from false gods, but from the real God. She continued to listen.

"Kristal, have you ever wanted something so badly that nothing would get in the way of it?"

She shook her head no. She did not dream; she did not allow them. That way there would never be any disappointment of her dreams not coming true. "Rodrigo had dreams and look what happened to them," she said softly.

El Padre looked at her sympathetically.

Kristal waited a few seconds. "No"—she felt the little bit of optimism she had starting to fade—"I do not have dreams."

"This might be part of God's plan. Maybe He wants to give you a dream, Kristal."

She looked down. "A dream? Why would He do that?" She looked at some stray pencil marks on the surface of the table.

"Because, Kristal, God loves you."

She continued to look down.

"He knows everything about you."

"Everything? Does He know that Rodrigo is the one who wants to be here?"

He shook his head yes. "But even so, I think you are the one who is supposed to be here."

She wondered why he would say that and shook her head in disagreement.

"Don't be so quick to say no," he said. "It's crazy how God works. A lot of times we never understand His plans until it's all over, and then we realize 'Wow! I guess God knew what He was doing after all!' I never understand why we question Him, but I do it all the time," he stated, honestly.

Even el Padre has doubts? thought Kristal.

He continued. "But then I realize that He is the source of our hope, Kristal. He gives us dreams. But you have to ask Him."

Dreams, she thought. *I've never asked for a dream before.* She looked up.

El Padre looked her intently in the eyes. "Kristal, hope is to believe in something bigger than you can ever imagine. Our God is that big, and He's capable of some very big things."

Kristal did not imagine much. She didn't think about much more than past the start of the next day.

He continued, "There is peace in believing. Believing that your Mamá will be healthy again. Believing that your Tío will heal from the explosion and will not have any more pain. Believing that Javier will grow up to be strong. Believing in dreams, Kristal, is good. It's good! You must allow yourself to have dreams, Kristal. Your brother, Rodrigo, has dreams. He has that hope. I didn't have to tell him where his hope comes from. He already knew. It was already burning inside his heart. What is your dream, Kristal? What is your hope?"

"My hope is if I believe like Rodrigo, that I am not loco."

"You will not be crazy, Kristal," he said, reassuringly. "When you believe, your heart opens, and you begin to dream big dreams." Kristal looked up at him. "Big dreams, Kristal," he emphasized.

Kristal felt emotion building up inside her. She felt confusion and anger and helplessness all at once. Feeling overwhelmed and no longer able to hold back her emotion, she blurted out, "I want to share in Rodrigo's dream. I want Mamá to have a casa where she can get healthy and where it is not so difficult for Javi to get around. A casa where we wouldn't have to sleep on a muddy dirt floor. A casa that has a roof that is not rusty or has holes." Feeling lighter, like she just took off a backpack with ten loads of potatoes, she started to cry. She cried like she had never cried before. Emotion seemed to run out of her pores. Because she was the oldest, she had held back her emotion for years. Years of worry for Mamá. Worry for food. Worry for the family. That day, it all came out.

"That is a beautiful dream, Kristal. It is not loco at all, as long as we ask it in His name," said el Padre, smiling. "Can I pray for you?"

She nodded. No one has ever prayed for her before.

"Lord, please hear Kristal's request. Help her Mamá feel better. Heal Tío. Help Javier get stronger, and Lord, please help Rodrigo's dream become a reality. Please help them to get a new home." He stood up and walked over to her side of the table, put his hand on her shoulder, and gave it a squeeze. "If you ever need to talk about anything, I am here."

"Thank you, el Padre." Kristal got up to leave.

Not bad for her first day of school, he thought. "See you tomorrow."

"Yes. Tomorrow," she said with a smile, and she walked home with Marissa.

NO LANGUAGE BARRIERS

The walls went up quickly. The father, and soon-to-be homeowner, helped as much as possible. He proudly held boards or dug holes for posts while Carlos and Pedro watched on, making sure not to get in the way. The boys knew exactly how close they could get to the work site by catching their mother's watchful eye. The team gave the boys their scrap wood, which kept them busy for hours. The boys had races using small boards as race cars. They made race-car noises, and Mandi thought imaginary Guatemalan race cars sound much like imaginary American race cars. The boys built towers

Team catching some shade for a rest as the structure of home starts to really take shape.

as high as they could stack the blocks and knocked them over with a crashing sound. They stacked the scrap wood and with a sizable broken limb of a nearby tree, they made a teeter-totter. Life was simple and sweet and hard. Mandi relished it.

By day three, people started getting used to seeing these not-so-strange strangers come every day. The team interacted more

Member of the team, Katrina Hatch, assisting another team member, Trey Brakefield, lifting tin up for the roof.

with the family and with those watching their neighbors' house being built. Mandi watched as one of her teammates, Miriam, took a break and played with some of the children. Miriam, Julie's younger sister, knew nothing of their language, not one word, yet they followed her like little chickens, with her as the mama hen. They played "Follow the leader." When she hopped, they hopped. When she danced on one foot, they danced on one foot. They followed her every move. When she clapped, they clapped. She clapped her hands, making rhythms, and the children copied. Mandi and Julie were next to each other, installing some trim around one of the windows. Mandi shook her head and said to Julie as they watched Julie's sister interact, "Sometimes no words can speak volumes."

Julie shook her head in agreement. "Hey, I'm really glad you came on this trip, Mandi. It's been great reconnecting."

"Me too," said Mandi. "I've really had a great time. I feel like we are being sort of Jesus-like."

Julie looked at her, inquisitively.

"You know . . . Jesus was a carpenter . . . we are being carpenters."

Julie nodded her head, then laughed. "Guess what. Our trim is about two inches too small."

"Looks like Jesus was a much better carpenter than us," Mandi remarked.

"Well, pretty sure he had connections."

"You're right on that one. Hey, I'm going to take a few pictures. I'll be right back."

Rodrigo and Javier were watching it all from their house. As they were rolling wicks for fireworks, they talked. "I am happy that Kristal's first day of school went well. That was a smart idea you had, Javi." As Rodrigo messed up Javi's hair, he added, "And you didn't even go to school." They both laughed. "But you will too someday. And you will be able to walk there."

"I hope so," said Javier with a nod.

"Come on, Javi, let's take a break." Rodrigo and Javier took a break from rolling fire wicks and joined the other children in watching their neighbor's house being built. The lady with the camera came up to them and took a photo.

"That is what I look like?" Javier asked Rodrigo.

Rodrigo looked at it too and laughed. "Javi, you are guapo, no?"

"I want to go tell Mamá," Javi said excitedly.

Two local kids having fun in front of the camera.

"She sees you every day. She knows what you look like."

"Yes, but she needs to see excitement. It makes her happy." As Javier ran back to his house to tell Mamá, he shouted behind him to Rodrigo, "I'll race you back!"

Mandi watched Javier hobble quickly as he negotiated his legs to move through the hard mud and ruts on legs that were not meant for this kind of terrain. Mandi's heart went out to him. Her heart went out to the family. As Javier glanced behind him to see if Rodrigo was gaining, she took a photo capturing his determined look.

"I'm going to catch you, Javi!" Rodrigo said as he ran, closing the gap, but making sure it wasn't enough to pass his brother. At the house, Rodrigo said, "I almost caught up to you!"

Javier proudly smiled. "Yes, I am getting much faster."

Javier's leg and back still hurt from the explosion, but through his excitement, he barely noticed any pain. In fact, it almost seemed as if the explosion had caused something in his left leg to get stronger. He was noticing more movement in his leg that he didn't have before the explosion. He didn't tell anyone yet; he didn't want to scare them. "Mamá!" he said excitedly as they got close to their house. "Mamá! I just saw a photo of Rodrigo and me. I am very guapo, Mamá!" he said grinning. "That is what the nice lady said."

"That you are, Javi," said his Mamá and she smiled. She had started on lunch. Tortillas and stewed tomatoes. With her hands full of sticky masa dough, she used her forearm to scruff Javier's hair. Mamá added, "And you, Rodrigo, are guapo, too." She saw him chasing Javier and knew Rodrigo let him win. She looked him in the eyes and smiled as if to say you are a great older brother. He saw the look and knew what she'd meant. The wind shifted and the smoke from the cooking fire made her cough.

Rodrigo patted her back to help stop the coughing and fanned the fire so the smoke would shift. As her cough subsided, he looked up the way and saw the team working hard. "Not much longer and their house will be complete," he said.

Mamá looked up and agreed.

"I wish it would be us, Mamá. Someday, Mamá, I will get you a house too."

Mamá looked him in the eyes. "Rodrigo, you work hard for the family and I love you. But, sometimes, it doesn't matter how hard we work. If it is God's will, it will happen."

"Then is there some way we can get on His list?"

"Just pray, Rodrigo. Just pray."

Just pray? To Rodrigo, that just didn't seem like enough. Surely, there was more than just that. *Am I starting to get like Kristal?* He was starting to understand why she always worried about their next meal. There was a lot to worry about when you don't get to leave the house. Mamá was his biggest concern. Her coughing never got any better.

As the sun made its way overhead, sweat soaked their clothes, sticking to their bodies. Mandi's jeans got heavier as the morning sun got stronger. She looked at the salt outline of sweat on a team-mate's T-shirt. It resembled the whole state of Texas, she thought. The father dropped off a watermelon at midday, and the team devoured every piece, appreciating the break and the energy it offered. Mandi was wishing she still had some of that energy now that it was afternoon. The area smelled of sunscreen and sweat and smoke

Team taking their well deserved late morning "watermelon break."

from the fire pit. Off to the side, the mother was preparing lunch. Tortillas again. Miriam, who was clapping hands with the kids earlier, came over to the mother. "Can you show me how to make tortillas?" She pointed to the masa. "I make?" she asked, simplifying her English, as if the woman understood her language. Pointing to the masa, Miriam asked again only slightly louder as if to think saying it louder would help her understand. "I make?" The mother put her hand to her mouth and shyly giggled. Mandi watched through her lens; she *did* understand. Julie was watching too. The mother did not understand the words, but understood what she meant. She nodded yes and explained how to cup her hand to get the right amount of masa and how to pat it so it would flatten correctly between the palms of her hands.

"Oh, I get it," said Miriam, nodding. Neither one knew the other's language, but it didn't matter. Somehow, they communicated. She explained through motions how to cook the tortilla on the flat tin pan, spin it on the pan so it wouldn't stick, and flip it over using only her hands. Miriam tried to flip the tortilla with her fingers. "Oh! That's hot!" she said as she blew on her fingers to cool them off.

Julie, looking at Mandi, said jokingly, "She got the looks, not the brains of the family."

Mandi laughed.

The mother "understood" and flipped it for her. Miriam smiled and asked, "Doesn't that hurt?" The mother laughed, not exactly sure what she just said, but somehow they worked out a silent deal. Miriam would pat the tortillas and put them on the tin and the mother would flip them.

"Good teamwork," said Mandi, behind her camera lens.

Miriam made a goofy smile and tried to get the mother to smile too, but she just looked at Miriam and giggled.

El Padre stopped by every day to talk with the team leader from Casas por Cristo and to see how the house was progressing. He greeted the neighbors he knew and smiled at the ones he didn't know. He stopped by to check on Rodrigo's family to see how Mamá,

Unbelievable beauty contrasted against unbelievable poverty.

Javi, and Tío were doing. He saw Mandi, who was resting at the edge of the hill, and walked up to greet her.

"Hey there," she said to el Padre. Taking a deep breath, she pointed to the horizon. "Sure is beautiful, isn't it? "

Looking at the scenery, he nodded. "I love the view from here."

"So what brings you here?" she asked, looking like she'd been thinking for a while.

He looked at her, questioningly. "Here, as in here, today? Or, here, as in Guatemala?"

"Guatemala."

"Well, since I already know your story, I guess I can tell you mine. Better get comfortable," he said, and he sat down next to her. "Well, I had been working in youth ministry all through college and continued on after I graduated, but for some reason I was getting itchy to do something different. I was twenty-seven and didn't know if that was what I wanted to do anymore.

"So, you sort of hit a crossroad?"

"Exactly. I saw an ad looking for missionaries in Guatemala for the summer, and for some reason, I felt like I was being called here. So, after discussing it with my family and friends, I knew that's what I was going to do—go to Guatemala to teach at the local school and help disadvantaged youth. I took a three-month leave of absence and said I'd see them all soon."

"What did your family think of that?"

"Well, they weren't too happy at first. Guatemala is pretty far away from Tennessee. But they understood the calling. If that's what God wanted, what could they do?"

Mandi nodded and listened. "Three months. Well, what happened? 'Cause I'm pretty sure you've been here longer than that."

"Right. Well, when I got here, the kids knew I worked in ministry, so they started calling me el Padre, and even though I'm not a pastor, the name stuck."

"Wait. You're not a pastor?" she asked, surprised.

"Technically, no.

"What does 'technically no' mean? I thought el Padre means 'the father.'"

"It does, but I really got the name because I love all the kids. I'm like the father that many of these kids don't have. What I did as ministry work was write curriculum for the students, and I did go to seminary for a year, but that didn't pan out either. That's why I'm working at the school. My degree is in education, and the curriculum I was writing was for disadvantaged youth. What better place to test it out than here in Guatemala?"

Mandi nodded in affirmation. "How did it work?"

"Well, disadvantaged here is a different level of disadvantaged than in the States. There's more of a distinction in the States."

She looked at him questioningly.

Clarifying his thought, he added, "There's more of a distinction of classes. In Guatemala, most people would be considered disadvantaged."

She nodded, listening as he continued.

"When I got here, I just fell in love with the kids . . . every one of them."

"I totally understand that," said Mandi. She had seen Pedro playing with Carlos on the teeter-totter made of a broken limb. Pedro would try hard to move the teeter-totter down fast so as Carlos went in the air, he would raise a few inches off the limb and nearly fall off. Pedro caught Carlos off guard and as he landed, he fell off to one side and slowly fell over. Once Carlos slid over, he fell off, making Pedro crash to the ground. The boys giggled so hard that Pedro fell off too.

El Padre continued. "So after my three months were done, I reluctantly got things ready to pack. In my heart, I knew my work here was not done, but my time was up. On my last day of school, I knew saying good-bye would be tough. But I didn't know how tough." His legs were stretched out in front of him as they talked. He crossed them the other way, leaning back on his arms. He looked at Mandi. "There was one little girl. Her name was Amelia." He paused for a second, reflectively. "She looked up at me with these huge, dark brown eyes with crocodile tears streaming down her face and asked, 'If you leave, who will teach us, el Padre?' Her voice cracked when she asked. My heart just twisted."

"Oh, I bet that was gut wrenching."

"Yeah," he chuckled, "my heart crumbled. I looked at Amelia and knew right then it would be me. I would be the one teaching them. That was five years ago. Guatemala is home now."

There was pounding in the background; the last of the boards for the walls was going up. Mandi pointed to all of the eyes watching the new home being built and asked, "From all the families here, who decides which of them gets a home? Everybody here is poor. Everybody is living in the same conditions." She nodded towards the house further down. "Like the family down there. We see that family every day and it breaks my heart. The kids peek their heads around the plastic sheet and they smile at us. The mother does not look healthy. They have a boy with a handicapped leg. And there is a man that has bandages all over his hands and face."

El Padre nodded. "Yes, they are the Manuela family. They are special to me. The fireworks factory had an explosion two weeks ago, and their uncle and the little boy, the one with the crippled leg, were there when it happened."

"Are they OK?" she asked, concerned.

"I've spoken with the family. The boy is remarkably fine. The explosion shot him in the air about twenty feet. The doctor is saying that the explosion may have done something to his leg to actually help him. The injury may have fused something together so his leg may start growing again. It's the craziest thing."

"That is crazy."

"The uncle, on the other hand, is healing slowly. Time will only tell for him. He had a lot of injuries, and they are thinking he will be blind. The older Manuela son, Rodrigo, used to attend the school where I teach. He's got a little place in my heart too. He's another Amelia. He was there for only about a couple of weeks before he had to quit, but he has such a passion to learn, such a passion to do more with his life." He paused and shifted his legs, crossing them Indian-style. "His uncle cannot work right now, so Rodrigo had to quit school in order to help make a living for the family. I was very sad for Rodrigo when he left. Sad for him and sad for his family. He was so excited to be there." He paused for a second and looked at Mandi. "He has a passion that I haven't seen in many of the Guatemalans here. His sister is now coming to the school. She doesn't share his passion, but she's made remarkable progress in the few days she's attended. They've had many hardships, but they're strong. Like all people here, they're strong." Mandi could see his passion for Guatemalan people. "When these teams show up, it offers them hope, Mandi. People come from across the world to build a home for them. They just think that's the most amazing thing that someone would come from another part of the world and build them a home. They could choose to go anywhere, but they choose to come here . . . *here*." He looked around at the poverty. "They wonder why anyone would help them. Especially people who don't even know them. I explain it's not really our choice, that God tells us to do things, and we obey." Mandi listened and could see his passion. "We are called to be His hands and feet. Sometimes people understand, sometimes they don't, but to see God's Word lived out is so exciting."

Mandi's heart stirred. Seeing God's word lived out . . . *maybe I didn't come here just to do a good deed. Maybe there was more to it.* Had she not come on this trip, Mandi would have had no idea what el Padre was talking about. *Seeing God's word lived out . . . what did that mean?* But, she was seeing it now. She understood. She could feel a strange love filling her heart, something different, a passion for people she'd never felt before. It was like a direct line into the flow of God's love. It was all very confusing and very conflicting and very amazing. Looking at the house they were building, she noted it was quite simple: cement floor, four walls, a couple of windows, a door with a lock, rudimentary electrical, and a tin roof. The inside was divided in half lengthwise, and made into two bedrooms. The other half was open.

"These four walls," el Padre explained, "are the start of a new life, the answer to someone's prayers. It is hope for a future."

Sitting there, Mandi thought of all the stuff she had in her life and how meaningless it all became. She thought of the many times she complained about being stuck in traffic, that she had mountains of laundry to wash or endless dishes to load into the dishwasher, that she needed to get some new clothes because she was bored with what was in her closet, or that she had to work instead of being able to go out with her friends. *That she had to work!* Looking around, she was almost ashamed that she would even think such a thought. She had a job. A very good job. She had a car. It was new. She had an apartment. It had a door with a lock and carpet on the floor. It had running water, electricity, and a bed. With a pillow and clean blankets. She had a machine to wash her laundry and her dishes. She was warm at night. She was safe. A tear ran down Mandi's face as she watched Carlos and Pedro giving high fives to the team. Mandi took a deep breath and smiled.

Seeing the tear, el Padre asked, "Are you OK?"

"Yes, just conflicted." Looking around, her voice cracked. "We have so much."

He understood and smiled. "It only took you a couple of days. God is showing you what breaks His heart. It took me a couple of weeks to see it. Guess I'm just slow."

They both laughed, and Mandi wiped away her tear.

"The greatest gift we can give is not the house that we are building, but the hope that it provides." He gave her shoulder a squeeze and got up. "Break's over," he said as he dusted off his pants.

"See you later," said Mandi, as she headed back to the site with her heart crumbling.

Off to the side, Mandi noticed Carlos and Pedro eyeing her hammer. Although they wanted to use it, they would not dare ask or touch until it was offered to them. Mandi handed Pedro her hammer and smiled. His eyes lit up and he said a whole bunch of words that she was sure meant thanks. Carlos found some of the bent nails in the dirt and together, the boys took turns pounding nails into boards. Mandi took a deep cleansing breath and got back to work, helping out with the board-cutting station. Julie gave her some measurements so Mandi could mark some of the boards to give to the cutter.

"Want to cut?" the person asked.

"Are you kidding? I'm dangerous with a hammer. No telling what I could do with a saw," said Mandi. "Thanks, but I think I need to stick with the pencil and tape ruler."

Julie nodded in agreement.

"Thanks for that support, Julie," said Mandi, starting to wrestle with the tape measure. The ruler wouldn't come out. Julie laughed and showed her how to unlock it. It reminded Mandi of their days in high school when Julie would play pranks on her.

The kids love to play with the wood scraps. Finding bent nails on the ground, they would straighten them out and try to build their own structures. They loved to help.

As the day came to an end, Mandi looked for the boys and went to get her hammer. They came over to her, excited about something they were holding behind their back. She looked at them inquisitively. "What is it?" she asked, wondering what they had been up to.

Pedro returned the hammer to her then pulled the surprise out from behind Carlos's back. They had built a small house out of the scrap boards. She looked at it as they handed it to her. Beaming, Pedro proudly said, "You build us a house. We build you a house." Mandi's eyes welled up with tears.

She touched her heart as if to say thanks. The boys smiled even bigger.

8

DAY OF CELEBRATION

The last day of the build is reserved for two things: the final details—activities like installing the panes on the windows, finishing the tin roof, installing the interior walls, and installing a lock on the front door—and the dedication ceremony.

Excitement was in the air. As Mandi looked around, she took a deep breath.

"The house is starting to look like a home," said Julie to Mandi. The roof was on, the windows and trim installed, walls were nearly up, and the electrical was nearly complete.

"Sure is" said Mandi, feeling a sense of accomplishment.

"Anyone want to help me install the door lock?" asked the site leader.

"As long as it's not with a saw, I think I can help." She followed him to the door. As she got the doorknob out of the box, something had occurred to her. "So, this family has probably never had a real door before. Or . . . a lock."

"You're right," he said. "They probably have never had a lock. Probably never needed one since they don't have anything to guard."

The thought saddened her. Just then, Carlos and Pedro ran by. "Nothing to guard but their family," said Mandi, in a heavyhearted tone.

"Yeah," agreed the site leader. "But they've got one now." He stood up and smiled at her. "So, do you want to know how today works?"

"Sure," she said, happy to change the topic to something more uplifting.

"Usually, teams finish around noon, and the local pastor comes to help with the dedication ceremony. El Padre usually comes too, to help out with translating. Afterwards, the family usually provides either a cake or a celebratory meal for the team. Can you hand me the hinge?"

She handed it to him, and he continued. "The celebratory meal is never mandatory, but it is very special." They installed the hinges to the door, and he continued, "The family has no way to repay the team for what they have done, but they want to do something special in return," he said, as he fanned out his hand towards the house. "The meal is the only offering they can provide."

Mandi could feel the excitement mounting, not just with the team, but also with the family. This was their big day, the day it was all finished, the day that Pedro and Carlos would have a home. No longer would they sleep on the dirt; they would now sleep on their mats on the cement. It would be dry, it would be clean, it would be home—their casa. They lavished in the joy of the day. It was their day.

As they wrapped up the final details on the house, the mother gathered up the boys and got them cleaned up. Carlos, Pedro, and their mother went to the water station, where the women washed clothes, and lined up children to wash their hair. Carlos did not like baths, but on this day, he didn't complain, not even once—another thing on his mother's list of reasons to be thankful for on this day.

The water station was rectangular with several cement sinks linked together, surrounded by one large water area in the middle. The women would go to one of the sink areas and do their laundry, and the children would line up at the end to wash their hair. The water was not drinkable or warm, but it was clean enough. Pedro's mother washed behind his ears and gave him the scrap cloth so he could do the rest of his body. Then it was Carlos's turn. They put on clean T-shirts and their nicest looking jeans. Pedro's jeans were getting a little small, but they were his best, and they were clean, so he put them on. Carlos rolled up the bottom of his pants and pulled them up every couple of minutes.

Once back at the new house, his father gave Carlos a rope, his new belt, to tie around his waist to keep his pants from slipping down. The boys waved to Mandi when they returned and said something to her. She did not know what they said, but she responded with "que guapo" (how handsome), happy that she has picked up a little Spanish on this trip. She watched their smile slowly fade as their mother said something to them. The gesture was universal to all languages—do not get dirty! Mandi laughed and gestured at the boys with her fingers, scolding them. They smiled back.

The mother and sister-in-law put on their finest Mayan embroidered clothes, and the father and oldest son put on clean checkered shirts. They had bathed earlier. Everyone was clean and ready.

Mandi and the team leader were still talking and working on installing the door. "To prepare, the woman of the house normally asks all the families nearby if she can borrow their plates and glasses so they can have the finest china to offer at this big event," he explained.

"So that's what the boys were doing," said Mandi, wondering what the boys were doing earlier. "I saw the boys gathering up cup and plates earlier and bringing them to their mother. The cups and plates kept coming in but not out."

He nodded. "The plates are chipped and match no other plates in the stack, but it's an honor to eat on them. You will see," he said, checking the lock. "Done." Looking around, he added, "Looks like we're just about ready for showtime."

El Padre showed up, along with the local pastor. Mandi waved to them. As the site leader walked around the house and checked the final details, the team gathered up tools and cleaned up the area. Someone made a string of balloons and hung it over the patio. It looked like the party was about to start. When the site leader gave the nod to the pastor indicating they were done, the team members were called together with the family so the dedication ceremony could begin.

Clouds were gathering, and everyone hoped it would not rain on the best part of the week, the dedication. Everyone gathered around the house. The family was off to the side, next to the pastor. The pastor thanked God for the marvelous day, a day that marked the start of a new life for this ever-thankful family. El Padre helped translate for the pastor and the team. "Gracias, Padre Dios." Immediately following his words, el Padre repeated, "Thank you, Father God." He thanked God

Group praying at the dedication service. The family, not shown, is on the front porch of their new home on the left.

for the weather; he thanked God for safety. Swept away with emotion of this moment, the pastor began to weep. The pastor thanked the team for leaving their families to go where God sent them and asked God to bless them. "Dios," he said, "gracias for the people who obediently answered your call to be your hands and feet."

Before this trip, Mandi had not understood "hands and feet." She smiled to herself and chuckled at the thought of her conversation with el Padre. A good deed. El Padre was right. It was a start, but she realized now it was way more than that. She felt it. She felt the flow of God's love and knew that this is what it's all about.

Pedro stood next to Mandi. He reached for her hand and was beaming, excited for what would soon be theirs. Silently, Mandi prayed. *Thank you God for letting us be a part of this.* Her crumbling heart found comfort as she squeezed Pedro's little hand. *There is no better joy than this.*

Julie and her sister presented the Bible to the family. They handed the father the Bible and said a few words. As Julie spoke, el Padre repeated, "Keep this Bible in the center of your house, as He is the center of our lives. Talk to him for all your needs, and He will provide. He will answer your prayers."

The family nodded, and the father looked at the house. "He has already answered our prayers." He took a deep breath, trying to quell the emotion that was inside him. "This is the first book I have ever owned." He took another deep breath. "It is the only book in this house, and it will be the foundation for my family." He softly and humbly added, loud enough for God to hear, "Thank you. Thank you, God, for answering my prayer."

Mandi presented the new owners with the keys to the house. She was honored. As she presented the keys to the father, they were all doing their best to control their emotions. Her voice cracked, and she took a deep breath. "God asked us to come here to build you a house." As Mandi spoke, the translator continued, " . . . to build you a place for you to raise your children . . . to build you a place that is safe for them . . . to build you a place for hope." Kristal, Rodrigo, and Javier were listening off to the side, soaking it all in. "God answers prayers . . . and we are honored and humbled to be part of your prayers." She could barely speak the words as she handed the keys to the father. She took a deep breath, and when she hugged the family, Mandi truly felt God's presence. That day, Mandi had her "defining moment."

The last thing to be done on the house, and the final step before the celebratory meal, was to nail up the metal placard that read *Casas por Cristo*. Each placard is numbered, to show how many "Houses for Christ" have been built. The placard read 14033.

"Wow, over fourteen thousand families impacted." Mandi couldn't

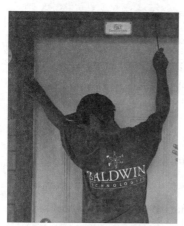

The new homeowner nailing in the last nail. He had to stop twice while hammering to wipe his tears away. Naturally, everyone else did the same.

imagine her heart being able to take it that many times. She could barely make it through this one.

One of the team members nailed in one side, started the nail on the other side of the placard, and moved out of the way for the father to pound the final nail into his very own home. The father looked up at the placard and wiped away a tear. As is typical of most Guatemalans, they are strong but not very tall. The father of the house could not reach the top of the door. He looked up for a few seconds, then someone from the team brought over a large bucket for him to stand on and, tipping it over, said, "Here. You can use this."

The father smiled and stood on the bucket. He took a deep breath. He did his best to hammer it in, but got as far as getting the nail started before he needed to stop. As tears clouded his view, he took

Jerry Hatch presents keys to the homeowner's new home at the dedication ceremony. It is always an emotional event, not only for the homeowner but also for those building the home. God's glory shows up big on those days.

a moment to collect his emotions. This was a big day for his family, a very emotional day. Tears blocked his vision, and after a couple of deep breaths, he was able to line the hammer up to the nail. The team, also weeping, cheered when he took the last swing with the hammer, pounding the last nail in his new home firmly in place.

Pedro had never seen his father cry before, as Mayan people do not generally show much emotion. Crying doesn't change things, his mother had told him many times, but he understood this was a different kind of crying. He looked up as a cloud covered the sun and for a couple of minutes, a small sprinkle of raindrops came down. As they touched his face, Pedro thought the raindrops might have come from the angels. Maybe they are crying happy tears too.

As everyone gathered for the meal the mother prepared, el Padre walked over to Mandi. "So, what do you think of all this?" he asked.

"It's very emotional," she said, still wiping away tears.

The mother of the new home making a chicken meal for the team that built them their new home. She flipped chicken above the coals using her bare hands. This meal cost around 3 week's salary for them. It was an honor and true celebration feast!

"It is. So, you think you'll be back next year?" Before she could answer, he added, "I just found out that we're going to have another build in this area, and you might find it to be pretty special."

Mandi looked up, inquisitive, but interested.

"Remember the Manuela family?" He nodded down towards their shanty. Mandi looked to where he pointed. Kristal was helping her mother make tortillas, while Rodrigo and Javi were helping Tío roll firecracker wicks. Tía was watching the young ones and washing laundry on a stone. "Yeah, them. I just found out the local pastors recently met, and they want us to schedule the Manuela family for next summer. Think the old ticker can handle another roller coaster ride?"

"Well, it's not that old" she smiled as she smacked him. "And I wouldn't miss it for the world."

Mandi and el Padre joined the team gathered around the old pink children's table that was used all week for the watermelon. The mother had covered it with a Mayan blanket on which she proudly served the special meal she had prepared. Mandi noticed there was one chicken missing from the pen.

9

HOPE LIVES HERE

It is Saturday, the day after the big celebration for the neighbors.

Kristal pulls back the black plastic sheet and sunlight dances on the dirt floor of her home. She sees their neighbor's new house above them. She watches the father read the Bible to his family as they all gather around him, listening intently. Carlos and Pedro are silently playing with the scrap boards left by the team. Kristal has finally listened to el Padre. She has begun to allow herself a dream, the same dream shared by Rodrigo, a dream that someday maybe they too would get a new home so Mamá could get better, so they could have a better life. Rodrigo is no longer concerned about Kristal going to school. She has vowed she will stay and he believes it. She actually likes el Padre; he is funny. In the short time she has been there, el Padre has taught her many things, but most of all, he's shown her what it's like to follow dreams. She likes the school and, best of all, she knows that having dreams is not "loco." Before dark every day, Kristal teaches Rodrigo and Javier the things that she learns in school.

"We will all be smart," says Javier, smiling.

"Javi, you are already smart," says Rodrigo. Javier knows what he means. How else would Kristal have ever gone to school?

Rodrigo continues to work in the fields and on rainy days helps Tío and Tía and Mamá roll firecracker wicks. He works hard to support his family.

Tío is slowly healing and hopes to get his bandages removed soon. The doctors say he will probably be blind in both eyes, but they are still hopeful that he might see. While his blindness may affect his sight, it will never affect his strength. Tío vows he will help Javier get stronger. "Javi, in my mind, you can run as fast as any shooting star. I may never see it for real, but I still know that it will happen."

Mamá still coughs, and the smoke from the fire still makes it hard for her to breathe. But now she shares Kristal's dream too.

As Kristal walks just past the cooking fire, she finds the place she calls her thinking place. From this spot, just on the other side of the cooking fire, she can see everything going on. She's been thinking lately that things are pretty good. She sits down and draws in a deep, contented breath. *Hope lives here*, thinks Kristal happily. *Hope lives here.*

Rodrigo sits down next to her, and rests his arm on her shoulder. Javier comes out too. Looking out in the distance, they can see someone briskly walking towards them. Squinting, Rodrigo asks, "Is that el Padre?"

Kristal focuses. "It is. Why would el Padre be coming here today? It is Saturday."

"I don't know," says Rodrigo, "but he looks excited about something."

Javi smiles. "I think I know what it is." They look at him as if to say "what," but Javi does not answer; he just smiles.

Catching his breath from the climb, el Padre greets the three of them. "I . . . have something . . . to tell you." They look at him, unsure what to think. He takes a couple of breaths. "Yesterday, you saw hope lived out for your neighbors. Go get your Mamá. I have some good news to tell her."

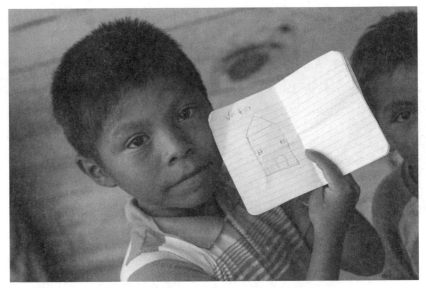

Victor, proudly holding up an illustration of his new home.

For more information about

Hope Lives Here

please contact:

www.facebook.com/HopeLivesHereBook

angela.hatch123@gmail.com

....

For more information about
AMBASSADOR INTERNATIONAL
please visit:

www.ambassador-international.com
@AmbassadorIntl
www.facebook.com/AmbassadorIntl

DATE DUE